Grammar Dimensions

Book 3B

Grammar Dimensions
Book 3B
Form, Meaning, and Use

Stephen H. Thewlis

American Language Institute
San Francisco State University

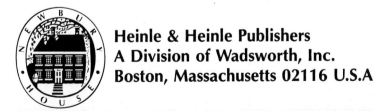

Heinle & Heinle Publishers
A Division of Wadsworth, Inc.
Boston, Massachusetts 02116 U.S.A

Photo Credits:

Photos on page 1, page 15 (top middle, top right, bottom middle), page 67, page 121, and pages 421–22 are courtesy of Pat Martin. Top middle photo on page 15 was taken at FlightStar, Champaign, IL; top right photo on page 15 was taken at Interior Galleries by Carter's, Champaign, IL; and photo on page 67 appears courtesy of Dr. Jan Colton.

Photos on page 2 (top) and page 107 appear courtesy of H. Armstrong Roberts.

Photo on page 2 (bottom) appears courtesy of NASA.

Photos on page 15 (top left, bottom left, and bottom right) appear courtesy of AP/Wide World Photos.

Photo on page 32 appears courtesy of Tennessee Wildlife Resources Agency.

Photo of Nazca Lines on page 46 appears courtesy of Paul Beals.

Photo of Stonehenge on page 46 appears courtesy of Robbie Edwards.

Photo on page 174 appears courtesy of Jessamine Santory.

Photo on page 181 appears courtesy of Florida Department of Natural Resources.

Photo on page 252 is United Nations Photo #123535, by Siceloff.

Photo on page 281 appears courtesy of Illinois Department of Transportation.

Photos on page 286 appear courtesy of Allen Bragdon.

Photo on page 339 appears courtesy of Sue Walton and Alan Thewlis.

The publication of the Grammar Dimensions series was directed by the members of the Heinle & Heinle ESL Publishing Team:

David Lee, Editorial Director
Susan Mraz, Marketing Manager
Lisa McLaughlin, Production Editor
Nancy Mann, Developmental Editor

Also participating in the publication of this program were:

Publisher: Stanley J. Galek
Editorial Production Manager: Elizabeth Holthaus
Assistant Editor: Kenneth Mattsson
Manufacturing Coordinator: Mary Beth Lynch
Full Service Production/Design: Publication Services, Inc.
Cover Designer: Martucci Studio
Cover Artist: Susan Johnson

10 9 8 7 6 5 4 3 2 1

Book 3B Table of Contents
(See page xii for Book 3A Table of Contents)

Book 3A Table of Contents

Preface to *Grammar Dimensions: Form, Meaning, and Use*

To the Teacher

ABOUT THE SERIES

With the recent emphasis on communication, the teaching of grammar has often been downplayed, or even overlooked entirely. Although one would not want to argue the goal of having students be able to communicate successfully, it is important to recognize that a major means to this end is to teach students to use grammatical structures. Some grammatical structures may be acquired naturally without instruction, but it is assumed by the creators of this series that explicit focus on the troublesome aspects of English will facilitate and accelerate their acquisition. The teaching needs to be done, however, in such a way that the interdependence of grammar and communication is appreciated.

In this regard, it is crucial to recognize that the use of grammatical structures involves more than having students achieve formal accuracy. Students must be able to use the structures meaningfully and appropriately as well. This series, therefore, takes into account all three dimensions of language: syntax/morphology (form), semantics (meaning), and pragmatics (use). The relevant facts about the **form, meaning,** and **use** of English grammatical structures were compiled into a comprehensive scope and sequence and distributed across a four-book series. Where the grammatical system is complex (e.g., the verb-tense system) or the structure complicated (e.g., the passive voice), it is revisited in each book in the series. Nevertheless, each book is free-standing and may be used independently of the others in the series if the student or program needs warrant.

Another way in which the interdependence of grammar and communication is stressed is that students first encounter every structure in a meaningful context where their attention is not immediately drawn to its formal properties. Each treatment of a grammatical structure concludes with students being given the opportunity to use the structure in communicative activities. The point of the series is not to teach grammar as static knowledge, but to have students use it in the dynamic process of communication. In this way grammar might better be thought of as a skill, rather than as an area of knowledge.

It is my hope that this book will provide teachers with the means to create, along with their students, learning opportunities that are tailored to learners' needs, are enjoyable, and will maximize everyone's learning.

ABOUT THE BOOK

This book deals with grammatical structures that ESL/EFL students often find challenging, such as the use of infinitives and gerunds. It also employs a discourse orientation when dealing with structures such as verb tenses and articles. Units that share certain features have been clustered together. No more than three or four units are clustered at one time, however, in order to provide for some variety of focus. As the units have been designed to stand independently, It is possible for a syllabus to be constructed that follows a different order of structures than the one presented in the book. It is also not expected that there will be sufficient time to deal with all the matieral that has been introduced here within a single course. Teachers are encouraged to see the book as a resource from which they can select units or parts of units which best meet student needs.

Unit Organization

TASKS

One way in which to identify student needs is to use the **Tasks**, which open each unit as a pre-test. Learner engagement in the Tasks may show that students have already learned what they need to know about a certain structure, in which case the unit can be skipped entirely. Or it may be possible, from examining students' performance, to pinpoint precisely where the students need to work. For any given structure, the learning challenge presented by the three dimensions of language is not equal. Some structures present more of a form-based challenge to learners; for others, the long-term challenge is to learn what the structures mean or when to use them. The type and degree of challenge varies according to the inherent complexity of the structure itself and the particular language background and level of English proficiency of the students.

FOCUS BOXES

Relevant facts about the form, meaning, and use of the structure are presented in **Focus Boxes** following the Task. Teachers can work their way systematically through a given unit or can pick and choose from among the Focus Boxes those points on which they feel students specifically need to concentrate.

EXERCISES

From a pedagogical perspective, it is helpful to think of grammar as a skill to be developed. Thus, in this book, **Exercises** have been provided to accompany each Focus Box. Certain of the Exercises may be done individually, others with students working in pairs or in small groups. Some of the Exercises can be done in class, others assigned as homework. Students' learning styles and the learning challenge they are working on will help teachers determine the most effective way to have students use the Exercises. (The Instructor's Manual should be consulted also for helpful hints in this regard.)

ACTIVITIES

At the end of each unit are a series of **Activities** that help students realize the communicative value of the grammar they are learning and that offer them further practice in using the grammar to convey meaning. Teachers or students may select the Activities from which they believe they would derive the most benefit and enjoyment. Student performance on these Activities can be used as a post-test as well. Teachers should not expect perfect performance at this point, however. Often there is a delayed effect in learning anything, and even some temporary backsliding in student performance as new material is introduced.

OTHER COMPONENTS

An **Instructor's Manual** is available for this book. The Manual contains answers to the Exercise questions and grammatical notes where pertinent. The Manual also further discusses the theory underlying the series and "walks a teacher through" a typical unit, suggesting ways in which the various components of the unit might be used and supplemented in the classroom.

A student **Workbook** also accompanies this book. It provides additional exercises to support the material presented in this text. Many of the workbook exercises are specially designed to help students prepare for the TOEFL (Test of English as a Foreign Language).

Each level of Grammar Dimensions is available in split editions (A and B) or as a complete text. The split editions are ideal for short courses or classes which move at a gradual pace.

To the Student

All grammar structures have a form, a meaning, and a use. We can show this with a pie chart:

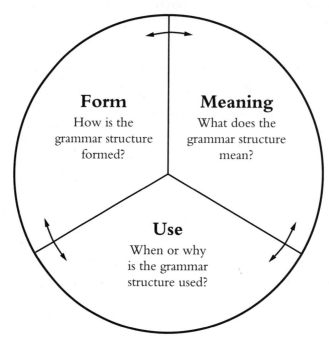

Often you will find that you know the answer to one or more of these questions, but not to all of them, for a particular grammar structure. This book has been written to help you learn answers to these questions for the major grammar structures of English. More importantly, it gives you practice with the answers so that you can develop your ability to use English grammar structures accurately, meaningfully, and appropriately.

At the beginning of each unit, you will be asked to work on a Task. The Task will introduce you to the grammar structures to be studied in the unit. However, it is not important at this point that you think about grammar. You should just do the Task as well as you can.

In the next section of the unit are Focus Boxes and Exercises. You will see that the boxes are labeled with **FORM, MEANING, USE,** or a combination of these, corresponding to the three parts of the pie chart. In each Focus Box is information that answers one or more of the questions in the pie. Along with the Focus Box are Exercises that should help you put into practice what you have studied.

The last section of each unit contains communicative Activities. Hopefully, you will enjoy doing these and at the same time receive further practice using the grammar structures in meaningful ways.

By working on the Task, studying the Focus Boxes, doing the Exercises, and engaging in the Activities, you will develop greater knowledge of English grammar and skill in using it. I also believe you will enjoy the learning experience along the way.

Diane Larsen-Freeman

Acknowledgments

Series Director Acknowledgments

As with any project this ambitious, a number of people have made important contributions. I need to thank my students in the MAT Program at the School for International Training and audiences worldwide for listening to me talk about my ideas for reconciling the teaching of grammar with communicative language teaching. Their feedback and questions have been invaluable in the evolution of my thinking. One student, Anna Mussman, should be singled out for her helpful comments on the manuscript that she was able to provide based on her years of English teaching. A number of other anonymous teacher reviewers have also had a formative role in the development of the series. I hope they derive some satisfaction in seeing that their concerns were addressed wherever possible. In addition, Marianne Celce-Murcia not only helped with the original scope and sequence of the series, but also provided valuable guidance throughout its evolution.

I feel extremely grateful, as well, for the professionalism of the authors, who had to put into practice the ideas behind this series. Their commitment to the project, patience with its organic nature, and willingness to keep at it are all much appreciated. I insisted that the authors be practicing ESL teachers. I believe the series has benefited from this decision, but I am also cognizant of the demands it has put on the authors' lives these past few years.

Finally, I must acknowledge the support of the Heinle and Heinle "team." This project was "inherited" by Heinle and Heinle during its formative stage. To Dave Lee, Susan Mraz, Lisa McLaughlin, and especially Susan Maguire, who never stopped believing in this project, I am indeed thankful. And to Nancy Mann, who helped the belief become a reality, I am very grateful.

Author Acknowledgments

To H. Douglas Brown, who pushed me into publishing. To my colleagues at the American Language Institute, who covered my bippy while I did it. To Diane (Sine qua non) Larsen-Freeman, for her guidance and direction in the development of the series, her great patience and flexibility, and her ability to find ways of keeping me busy and involved during the entire course of the project. To Nancy Mann for her extraordinarily sensitive perspective. To the teachers and students of the American Language Institute, who piloted the materials and made enormously helpful comments—especially Beth Erickson and Jennifer Schmidt.

To the reviewers of the manuscript, Janet Goodwin (UCLA), Patricia Brennecke (Harvard University), Corey Mass (Miami-Dade Community College), Paul E. Munsell (Michigan State University), Michael Calderado (Passaic Community College), Marlene Gross (Concordia College), Joseph Dunwoody (San Antonio College), Jack Ramsay (American University), and to Rita Silver, who class tested the manuscript at Boston University.

To the people, real and imaginary, who appear in these pages. And most especially to Michael Mercil, for his love, support, and patience all through this long, long sojourn in Grammarland.

17

Relative Clauses

Task

In 1943, two identical male twins were born in Ohio. Their mother wasn't married, so she gave the children up for adoption. They were separated the day after they were born, and grew up in different parts of the country, unaware of each other's existence. Neither one knew he had a twin brother until one twin moved to the same state where the other twin was living. Then friends began telling each of them that they had seen a man who looked just like him. The two men each began doing research and discovered their backgrounds and the fact that they were twins. They finally met each other in 1989.

Many researchers are interested in this case because they want to see if the two men have any similarities in spite of the fact that they have been raised in completely different environments. The researchers have found that there were, of course, many differences between the two men, but there are also some very intriguing similarities: They each had a blond wife and three children. They each had a yellow house. They both had dogs, and shared similar interests and hobbies. They both had jobs that called for a lot of travel.

Here is some information about one twin:

He has a modern ranch-style home.

His house is painted bright yellow.

He is married to a woman named Betty.

His wife has blond hair.

He has three children—all boys.

His eyes are each a different color.

He didn't tell his children that he had been adopted.

He sells plumbing supplies and his job involves a lot of travel.

He has a German shepherd named Prince.

His hobbies are stamp collecting and watching sports on TV.

His favorite beer is Miller.

He likes to play football.

Here is some information about the other twin:

He has an old-fashioned bungalow-style home.

His house is painted bright yellow.

He is married to a woman named Bernice.

His wife has blond hair.

He has three children—all girls.

His eyes are each a different color.

His children knew that he had been adopted.

He sells advertising space in magazines, and his job involves a lot of travel.

He has a poodle named King.

His hobbies are stamp collecting and watching sports on TV.

His favorite beer is Budweiser.

He likes to play basketball.

- Identify which characteristics both twins have and which are different. Use the information that describes the differences to answer the following questions with complete sentences. Start each answer with "The twin who...." Here is an example:
  Which twin is married to Bernice?
  The twin who has an old-fashioned bungalow is married to Bernice.

  Which twin has children that are all girls?

  The twin who _____

  Which twin owns a dog named Prince?

  The twin who _____

  Which twin told his children that he had been adopted?

  The twin who _____

  Which twin drinks Miller?

  The twin who _____

  Which twin prefers basketball?

  The twin who _____

  Which twin lives in a ranch-style home?

  The twin who _____

- Check the accuracy of your answers by comparing them with those of another student. Which information did each you use to identify the appropriate twin?
- Taking both the differences and similarities between the two men into account, discuss the following question with your partner and decide whether you think the answer is *yes* or *no*.

  Is there a relationship between genetic makeup and personality traits?

- Present your opinion and at least two pieces of information that support your opinion to the rest of the class.

Focus 1

Combining Sentences

FORM

- There are a number of structures that you can use to combine sentences in English:
  - **coordinating conjunctions** (see Unit 8):
    - **(a)** Jeff likes weight lifting. Matt likes weight lifting.
    - **(b) Both** Jeff **and** Matt like weight lifting.
    - **(c)** Jeff likes weight lifting, **and so does** Matt.
  - **subordinating clauses and phrases** (see Unit 13):
    - **(d)** Bambang Soetomo has decided to study in the United States. He wants an advanced degree in mechanical engineering.
    - **(e) In order to** get an advanced degree in mechanical engineering, Bambang Soetomo has decided to study in the United States.
    - **(f) Although** he is a little homesick, he still thinks his decision was a good one.
  - **relative clauses (embedding one sentence into another):**
    - **(g)** I visited an old friend last week after school. The friend lives in my apartment building.
    - **(h)** I visited an old friend **who lives in my apartment building** last week after school.
- Complex academic, technical, and literary prose generally tends to use embedding and subordination more often than coordinating conjunctions.

Exercise 1

Restate these combined sentences as two independent sentences. There may be more than one way to state the ideas, so compare your answers with those of other students in the class.

EXAMPLES: Both Biff and Gladstone are trying to improve their appearance.

Biff is trying to improve his appearance. Gladstone is trying to improve his appearance also.

Although John is a little homesick, he still plans to stay in France for at least a year.

John is a little homesick. He still plans to stay in France for at least a year.

I wrote to an old friend who went to school with me last night after dinner.

I wrote to an old friend last night after dinner. She went to school with me.

1. Jeff likes to get up early most days, but prefers to sleep late on weekends.
2. Denise has so much work to do to that she can't even consider taking a vacation.
3. Because they feel war is so destructive, many people are opposed to military solutions for international problems.
4. I once met a man who looked just like a friend of mine.
5. Bob is looking for a part-time job because he needs some extra money.
6. On Saturday mornings, I either clean the house or go shopping.
7. I know an old lady who swallowed a fly.
8. Although I have many friends, I still enjoy getting to know new people.

Focus 2

MEANING

Using Relative Clauses

- You can combine sentences by modifying any noun with a relative clause. You can use relative clauses
  - in affirmative and negative statements:
    (a) I have a friend **who likes opera.**
    (b) I don't know anyone **that can give you that information.**
  - in questions:
    (c) Do you know any doctors **that don't charge too much for an office visit?**
    (d) Where can I find a plant **that doesn't need much water?**
  - to modify nouns that are either subjects or objects in the main sentence:
    (e) Charley told me about a beautiful woman:
    - subject
      (f) The woman that Charley told me about is very beautiful.
    - object
      (g) Last night I met **the woman that Charley told me about.**
    - indirect object
      (h) I sent **the woman that Charley told me about** a long letter.
    - object of a preposition
      (i) I'm crazy about **the woman that Charley told me about.**
  - to modify an indefinite noun—give more information about it:
    (j) I read **a book that was written by your economics professor.**
    (k) I finally met **a person who likes classical Japanese music as much as I do.**
  - to identify a definite noun—make the noun specific:
    (l) I want to visit **the hotel that I read about in the newspaper.**
    (m) Please pass me **the notebook that has my name on it.**

Exercise 2

Underline each relative clause in this passage and circle the word it modifies. The first two have been done for you as an example.

(1)My friend Charley has fallen madly in love. (2)He says that he has finally met (the woman) that he has been looking for all his life. (3)He has always been attracted to (women) that are intelligent and independent, and who have a good sense of humor and a love of adventure. (4)The woman that he has fallen in love with has all those things and more, according to Charley. (5)Even though physical appearance isn't the most important characteristic that Charley is looking for, he is quite happy his new friend is attractive and athletic. (6)She not only runs and skis, but also goes skin-diving, and has several other interests that Charley also shares.

(7)Charley was never completely happy with the women that he used to go out with. (8)There was always something that he wasn't satisfied with. (9)I used to tell him that he was too fussy. (10)The "perfect woman" that he was looking for didn't exist. (11)No real person can equal the picture that someone has in his or her imagination. (12)But I'm glad he has found someone that he thinks is perfect. I've never seen him happier.

Focus 3

FORM

Forming Relative Clauses with Relative Pronouns

FORM

- The term for a noun that is modified by a relative clause is **head noun**. To form a relative clause, change the noun that repeats the head noun to a relative pronoun and move it to the front of the relative clause.

           head noun   **repeated element**
(a) I read **a book.** Charley really likes **it**.

            relative pronoun
(b) I read a book **that** Charley really likes.

- The relative pronouns are *who/whom*, *that*, and *which*. Use *who* and *whom* with humans. Use *which* with nonhumans. Use *that* for either.

(c) I met the *man who* you told me about.

(d) I read the *book which* Kevin had recommended.

(e) I met the *man that* you told me about.

(f) I read the *book that* Kevin had recommended.

Exercise 3

Replace the relative pronoun *that* with *who, whom,* or *which* in the following sentences.

(1)I finally met the woman that Charley has fallen in love with. (2)She seems to be the kind of person that likes being active and adventurous. (3)She has a responsible position in a company that produces computer programs. (4)That's a field Charley is also interested in. (5)She likes hobbies that involve athletics and being outdoors. (6)She seems to like all of Charley's friends that she has met so far, including me. (7)Maybe one of these days, I'll meet a woman that's like Charley's new girlfriend. (8)In the meantime, Charley had better hope that she doesn't meet a man that's like me! I just might try to ask her out myself!

Focus 4

FORM

Relative Pronouns
in the Relative Clause

FORM

- You can use relative pronouns to replace any noun or pronoun within the relative clause.

Underlying Sentence	Relative Clause
Subjects: (a) **The book** was published last year.	(b) I read the book **that** was published last year.
Objects: (c) Your professor wrote **the book.**	(d) I read the book **that** your professor wrote.
Indirect Objects: (e) Charley gave **the person** flowers.	(f) I met the person **that** Charley gave flowers to.
Objects of Prepositions: (g) Charley told me **about the person.**	(h) I met the person **that** Charley told me about.

- Remember that the replaced noun or pronoun of the underlying sentence does not appear in the relative clause.

(i)	I read the book **that** was published last year.	**(j)**	NOT: I read the book that **it** was published last year.
(k)	I read the book **that** your professor wrote.	**(l)**	NOT: I read the book that your professor wrote **it**.
(m)	I met the person **that** Charley gave flowers to.	**(n)**	NOT: I met the person that Charley gave **her** flowers.
(o)	I met the person **that** Charley told me about.	**(p)**	NOT: I met the person that Charley told me about **her**.

Exercise 4

In the following passage, circle the head noun of each relative pronoun *that, who, whom,* or *which*. Show the position of the replaced noun in the relative clause by drawing an arrow from the head noun to the place where the replaced noun has been removed.

EXAMPLE: I read (a book) that was published last year.

I read (a book) which your professor wrote.

I met (the person) whom Charley gave flowers.

I met (the person) who Charley told me about.

(1)I read an article the other day that interested me a great deal. (2)It reported on a survey that some sociologists conducted recently. (3)They examined the attitudes that American women have about men, and they identified some of the things that women consider to be important characteristics in a good husband or boyfriend. (4)The study determined that women seem to prefer men who can express their feelings. (5)Most women prefer husbands who they can talk to easily, and who they can share their problems with. (6)There were also several other things that women consider important in a partner. (7)A man's character or personality is more important to many women than the type of job that he has, or the amount of money that he makes. (8)Not surprisingly, most women want a husband that will take on an equal share of housekeeping and child-raising duties. (9)But the bottom line is this: Women want husbands who they can trust and depend on. (10)Unfortunately, more than 70 percent of the women who answered the questionnaires said they had husbands who did not meet these basic requirements in some way.

Focus 5

FORM

Deleting Relative Pronouns

FORM

- You can delete relative pronouns if they function as objects in the relative clause.
  - direct objects:
    - **(a)** I read the book **that** your professor wrote.
    - **(b)** I read the book your professor wrote.
  - indirect objects:
    - **(c)** The lady **that** Charley sent flowers is on the phone.
    - **(d)** The lady Charley sent flowers is on the phone.
  - objects of prepositions:
    - **(e)** I read the book **that** Charley was so excited about.
    - **(f)** I read the book Charley was so excited about.
- You can delete relative pronouns if they are in relative clauses with *be* as a main verb or auxiliary. In such cases, both the relative pronoun and *be* are deleted:
  - passive forms:
    - **(g)** I want a book **that was written** by an expert.
    - **(h)** I want a book **written** by an expert.
  - progressive forms:
    - **(i)** I think I know that woman **who is carrying** the blue suitcase.
    - **(j)** I think I know that woman **carrying** the blue suitcase.
  - prepositions:
    - **(k)** I tried to get an autograph from the baseball player **who is beside** the fence.
    - **(l)** I tried to get an autograph from the baseball player **beside** the fence.
  - adjective phrases:
    - **(m)** Anyone **who is** foolish enough to use drugs should be free to do so.
    - **(n)** Anyone **foolish enough** to use drugs should be free to do so.
- You cannot delete relative pronouns if they are subjects of a relative clause without **be.**
    - **(o)** Have you read the book **that** made Darryl Brock famous?
    - **(p)** NOT: Have you read the book made Darryl Brock famous?

Exercise 5

Delete the relative pronouns where possible and make the other necessary changes. (You cannot delete all the relative pronouns in this passage.) Prepare to explain your choices. The first paragraph has been done for you as an example.

(1)The kind of people ~~that~~ I like are usually people who have a good sense of humor. I like people who take other people's feelings into account, and people ~~who are~~ actively involved in making the world a better place.

(2)I like people who don't take themselves too seriously. (3)I find people who are lacking a sense of humor often tend to be pessimistic about many things. (4)A person who can't laugh at himself may not be able to distinguish between the things that are really important in life and the things in life that only seem important at the moment.

(5)I dislike people who strive to be important and powerful without also trying to be kind, fair, and helpful. (6)I dislike people who intentionally try to hurt other people's feelings. (7)People who are too concerned with their own power and position often try to take power from other people by making them appear or feel bad.

(8)I like people who think about important issues, such as the purpose of life and death or how to increase cooperation between different countries and people. (9)I prefer them to people who are only worried about the color that they want to paint their living room, or the kind of clothes that they would like to wear to a party that a friend is having next weekend.

(10)But I guess most of all I like people who are like me, and who also like me in return.

Exercise 6

Underline all the relative clauses in this passage. Make sure that you also include the ones that have deleted relative pronouns. The first two relative clauses have been done for you as an example.

(1)When World War I was finally over, it was called "The war to end all wars." (2)It was the most destructive war <u>the world had fought up to that time.</u> (3)Enormous numbers of young men <u>sent to battle from both sides</u> were killed or permanently crippled. (4)The war introduced weapons and techniques the world had never before seen. (5)The use of the airplane enabled armies on both sides to drop bombs with an effectiveness and precision that had been previously impossible. (6)Heavy casualties were also caused by the wide-scale use of a poison gas, called mustard gas, which permanently damaged the lungs of soldiers caught without gas masks. (7)There were more than 8.5 million casualties. (8)Most of these were people killed in action. (9)But many also died from intestinal diseases caused by the unsanitary conditions on the battlefield, or by infections that developed in lungs damaged by mustard gas.

(10)The peace established by "the war to end all wars" lasted less than a generation. (11)The most destructive war the world had ever known, like most wars, only provided a very temporary solution to the political and economic problems facing European governments at that time. (12)Just 20 years after the signing of the economically damaging treaty the winners had forced the losers to accept, Europe was again at war.

Focus 6

Differences Between Formal and Informal Usage

USE

- In formal English, use *who* as the relative pronoun for subjects in relative clauses. Use *whom* for objects in relative clauses.

  (informal) **(a)** This is the person Charley met at the party.

  (b) This is the person **that** Charley met at the party.

  (c) This is the person **who** Charley met at the party.

  (formal) **(d)** This is the person **whom** Charley met at the party.

- In formal written English, it is considered bad style to separate the preposition and its object. As a result, the preposition precedes the relative pronoun.

  (informal) **(e)** That's the situation I was so worried about.

  (f) That's the situation **that** I was so worried about.

  (g) That's the situation **which** I was so worried about.

  (formal) **(h)** That's the situation **about which** I was so worried.

- In such cases, you must use *whom* or *which*, instead of *that* or *who*.

  (i) That's the situation **about which** I was so worried.

  (j) NOT: That's the situation **about that** I was so worried.

  (k) That's the woman **about whom** Charley told us.

  (l) NOT: That's the woman **about who** Charley told us.

Exercise 7

Make these sentences more appropriate for formal written English by putting the preposition at the beginning of the relative clause:

EXAMPLE: Pollution is a problem people are just becoming concerned about.

Pollution is a problem about which people are just becoming concerned.

1. Charley has fallen in love with the woman his cousin introduced him to.
2. I no longer have a friend I can go to the movies with, now that Charley is spending all his free time with his new girlfriend.
3. World War I did not really provide a solution to the problems it was fought for in the first place.
4. Turkey was one of the countries Germany was allied with during World War I.
5. This is the article I told you about.
6. Women prefer husbands they can discuss their troubles and concerns with.
7. Some of the issues my friends are concerned about are environmental destruction, political activism, and developing alternative energy sources.

Exercise 8

Change the second sentence in each of these pairs into a relative clause and insert it into the first sentence. Delete the relative pronoun wherever possible.

EXAMPLE: Charley introduced the woman to his parents. He had been dating her for several weeks.

Charley introduced the woman he had been dating for several weeks to his parents.

1. Last month Charley fell in love with a young woman. He had been introduced to her by some mutual friends.
2. She had a number of positive characteristics. Charley found them quite attractive.
3. She was careful to leave time for other activities and interests. These helped keep her healthy, and reflected her commitment to the needs of her friends and family.
4. She had a wonderful sense of humor. This made their times together relaxing and enjoyable.
5. From the first time they met, Charley felt there was a "special understanding" between them. He was unable to explain it.

Focus 7

MEANING

Whose in Relative Clauses

MEANING

- When a relative clause contains a possessive form, you can use *whose* + **noun** in the same way that you use relative pronouns. You can use *whose* with
  - the subject of the relative clause:
    - **(a)** I met **a man. His house** was destroyed in the earthquake.
    - **(b)** I met a man **whose house** was destroyed in the earthquake.
  - the object of a relative clause:
    - **(c)** I got a letter from **a man.** We visited **his house** last week.
    - **(d)** I got a letter from the man **whose house** we visited last week.
  - the object of a preposition in a relative clause:
    - **(e)** I spoke to a man. We got an invitation **to his party.**
    - **(f)** I spoke to the man **whose party** we got an invitation to.
- You can never delete **whose** from a relative clause. It must always be used with a noun.
    - **(g)** I got a letter from the man **whose house** we visited last week.
    - **(h)** NOT: I got a letter from a man **house** we visited last week.
    - **(i)** NOT: I got a letter from a man **whose** we visited last week.

Exercise 9

Write the two underlying sentences that have been combined.

> **EXAMPLE:** I spoke to the man whose party we got an invitation to.
>
> *I spoke to a man. We got an invitation to his party.*

1. Bernice is married to the twin whose dog is named King.
2. The twin whose children are all girls told them about his background.
3. The children whose father didn't tell them that he had been adopted are all boys.
4. Betty is married to the twin whose dog is named Prince.
5. The modern ranch-style home belongs to the twin whose favorite sport is football.
6. Bernice is the wife of the twin whose friends first reported that they had seen his "double."
7. Twins whose upbringings are different still tend to have many characteristics in common.
8. People whose physical characteristics are identical also tend to have similar personalities and interests.

Exercise 10

Combine these sentences using *whose*.

> **EXAMPLE:** I got a letter from a man. We visited his house last week.
>
> *I got a letter from the man whose house we visited last week.*

1. Florence met a man. His twin brother is a well-known geneticist.
2. Jeff and Matt are roommates. Matt's nickname is "Akbar."
3. People may have similar personalities. Their genetic makeups are similar.
4. Joan took a class from a teacher. She knew his wife in college.
5. Mary Rae would like to go to the lecture by the mountain climber. She read about his latest climb in *Adventure Magazine*.
6. My friend has a dog. Its eyes are different colors.
7. I keep getting phone calls for some stranger. His last name is apparently the same as mine.
8. Charley finally succeeded in meeting the artist. He had been admiring her work for years.

Focus 8

Using *Whose* vs. *Of Which* in Relative Clauses

USE

- *Of which* can indicate possessive meaning in relative clauses instead of *whose*. Choosing the appropriate form depends on the head noun and the level of formality. You generally use *of which* to refer to
  - nonliving, physical objects:
    - **(a)** At the back of the restaurant was **a shabby wooden table.** The top **of the table** was incredibly dirty.
    - **(b)** At the back of the restaurant was a shabby wooden table, **the top of which** was incredibly dirty.
  - abstract concepts, characteristics, ideas:
    - **(c)** I read a novel, **the ending of which** was so shocking that I couldn't sleep after I finished it.
    - **(d)** Crete was a civilization, **the beginnings of which** are now lost in the mists of time.
- In formal writing and speech, *whose* usually refers to living (usually human) things. In informal writing, you can use *whose* for concepts, ideas, and so on, or even physical objects:
  - **(e)** This is the man **whose** book we were talking about.
  - **(f)** I read a novel **whose** ending was so shocking that I couldn't sleep after I read it.
  - **(g)** Crete was a civilization **whose** beginnings are now lost in the mists of time.
  - **(h)** That's the car **whose** owner lives next door.
- Because using *of which* seems very formal and using *whose* may seem illogical, writers try to avoid both *of which* and *whose* constructions when discussing abstract antecedents or physical objects. They more commonly express the same idea with different relative clauses or without relative clauses.
  - **(i)** The ending of the novel **(that)** I just read was so shocking that I couldn't sleep after I read it.
  - **(j)** **The beginnings of Cretan civilization** are now lost in the mists of time.
  - **(k)** That car **belongs to** my next-door neighbor.

Exercise 11

Combine these sentences using *whose* and *of which*. Decide how formal each choice is, and whether the informal version is logical or not. Then try to restate the ideas in a way that avoids the problem, by avoiding *whose* and *of which*.

EXAMPLE: Scientists have discovered a new disease. Its causes are still unknown.
               Scientists have discovered a new disease the causes of which are still unknown. (very formal)
               Scientists have discovered a new disease whose causes are still unknown. (informal—and a little illogical, since a disease is not a person)
               The causes of the new disease that scientists have discovered are still unknown. (possible restatement)
               Although scientists have discovered a new disease, they still don't know its causes. (possible restatement)

1. My brother bought a used car. Its tires need to be replaced immediately.
2. We'll be going to an opera. The synopsis of the opera can be found in the program.
3. I saw a mysterious-looking symbol. Its meaning was as mysterious as its design.
4. Darryl has finished his latest book. Its cover had his picture on it.

Focus 9

MEANING

Using *Where* and *When* in Relative Clauses

MEANING

- There are two relative adverbs *where* and *when*, which behave very much like *whose*.

Meaning	Sentences with Relative Adverbs	Implied Meaning
where Reference to *there* or prepositions meaning *in/on/at* that place.	**(a)** We arrived at a hotel **where** we were told we had no reservation.	We arrived at a hotel. We were told that we had no reservation **there.** We arrived at a hotel **at which** we were told that we had no room.
when Reference to *then* or to prepositions meaning *in/on/at* that time.	**(b)** Please come to my house at another time **when** I will be able to see you. **(c)** I can't remember a time in my childhood **when** I was completely happy.	Please come to my house at another time. I will be able to see you **then.** I can't remember a time in my childhood **during which** I was completely happy.

- You cannot delete *when* and *where*. Most writers prefer them over *at which* or *during which* for all but extremely formal contexts.

Exercise 12

Combine these pairs of sentences, using *when* or *where*.

> **EXAMPLE:** In yesterday's newspaper, I read about a demonstration.
> All the protesters blew whistles and stopped traffic at the demonstration.
> *In yesterday's newspaper, I read about a demonstration where all the protesters blew whistles and stopped traffic.*

1. My father can remember the old days. There were no televisions or computers in those days.
2. I'm going to start reading again. I stopped reading at the bottom of the page last night.
3. Jeff grew up in a small town in Kansas. Everybody there knew everybody else.
4. Most people think New Orleans is a great place. Everyone can live as they please there.
5. Do you remember that Halloween party at Alice's house? That evening everyone ran outside in their costumes and surprised the neighbors.

Exercise 13

Combine these numbered pairs of sentences in this paragraph, using *when* or *where*.

(1) The Sixties were a time of rapid social change. Many people explored alternative life-styles at that time. (2) The change was greatest in urban areas. There were a lot of young people studying at universities and colleges in those areas. (3) San Francisco was one center of the hippie movement. Many people gathered there during the famous "Summer of Love" in 1968. (4) The Haight-Ashbury was the center of activity. People from all parts of the city came to Haight-Ashbury to listen to rock and roll concerts. (5) People today look back upon the Sixties as an important time. Old values were brought into question, and people experimented with new answers at that time.

Exercise 14

Combine these numbered pairs of sentences in this paragraph, using *when* or *where*.

(1) We stayed at a hotel in Mexico. They had trained monkeys in the lobby of the hotel. (2) We arrived at the hotel during a festival. All the hotels in town were full during the festival. (3) Someone had put our reservation in the wrong file. No one else could find it in that place. (4) They put us in a very small room. There were no windows there. (5) Our vacation became much more pleasant on the next day. We were moved to a larger room on the next day.

Exercise 15

Combine these numbered pairs of sentences in this paragraph using *whose, where,* and *when* or *relative pronouns.*

(1)Charley wants to make some changes in his life. These changes involve both his life-style and his social activities. (2)Charley wants to find a new place to live. There is enough room for a dog. (3)He plans to move next year. The lease on his old apartment expires then. (4)He's looking at a new apartment. There is a balcony in the apartment, so he can grow some flowers. (5)Charley also wants to get married to someone. Her political beliefs are similar to his own. (6)He hasn't found anyone yet. No one seems to share his interest in politics and sports. (7)He often goes to coffee shops. People of similar interests go there on weekends. (8)He's thinking of putting a personals ad in a paper. A lot of people advertise in that paper in order to meet others with similar interests and backgrounds.

Activities

Activity 1

In Exercise 4, you read about some of the things that American women consider important in a husband. Divide into groups of men and groups of women. In your group, discuss the characteristics of **"the ideal spouse."**

- Prepare a list of 10–15 statements like these:

  "The ideal husband is someone who takes an equal responsibility for raising the children."

  "The ideal wife is a person who is able to maintain a good sense of humor."

  What ideals do you all agree on? Are there ideals that are controversial?

- Present your statements to the other groups. Compare the ideals presented by women's groups and the ideals presented by men's groups.

- Discuss these questions as a whole class or in groups of mixed sex: What are the important similarities and differences between the statements of the two kinds of groups? Are there some ideals that all men share, no matter what culture they come from? Are there some ideals that all women share, no matter what culture they come from? Are there some ideals that everyone shares, regardless of gender?

Activity 2

What kind of people do you like most? What personal characteristics do you appreciate and respect in other people? What personal characteristics do you find distasteful?

- Write a brief essay describing personal characteristics in people that you like and dislike. You may wish to look at the essay in Exercise 5 for some ideas about the kinds of characteristics other students have identified, and for an example of the kind of essay you should write.

Activity 3

The word *daffy* means "silly." A *daffynition* is a made-up definition for a word that doesn't really exist. In fact, the word *daffynition* is, itself, a made-up word. Try to invent daffynitions for these made-up words.

Here's an example: **Murphler:** A murphler is someone who makes a lot of noise when he eats.

Daffynitions:

Who or what is a **murphler**?

What do **parahawks** do?

What does **chemicophysiologicalistic** mean?

What do **flurps** and **mompsquats** have in common?

What are **quatchels**?

Define **hypervoraciosity**.

- Share your daffynitions with the rest of the class. The class should decide who has the most believable daffynition, and who has the most amusing daffynition for each term. Make up some of your own imaginary words and provide daffynitions for them as well.

Activity 4

A *pacifist* is someone who doesn't believe in fighting wars, under any circumstances. Are you a pacifist, or do you believe that there can be such a thing as a "justifiable" war? Is there a difference between a *war* and a *revolution*? Give some examples of armed conflicts that you feel were or were not justifiable. Under what circumstances is it acceptable to take up arms against your own government, other countries, or other groups of people within your own country?

Organize a debate between the doves (a slang term for pacifists) and the hawks (people who believe that wars are justifiable). You may wish to discuss the issues in terms of wars in general, or a specific conflict that you are familiar with (such as the Second World War, the Vietnam War, or the War in the Persian Gulf).

Activity 5

All languages have words that describe concepts or ideas that are not found in other languages. For example, in English the words *alone* and *lonely* have quite different meanings. One can be alone without being lonely, and lonely without being alone. But in many languages, these concepts are expressed by a single word.

- Choose a word from another language that you are familiar with that expresses a concept that doesn't exist in English, or that suggests a very different implication than its English counterpart.
- Present your word to the rest of the class, give a definition of it, and explain why you think that there is not a word for that concept in English.

Activity 6

In American English, we often make a "dramatic introduction" in certain formal situations. A dramatic introduction lists a person's characteristics and accomplishments and ends with the individual's name. Here's an example of a "dramatic introduction":

> Ladies and Gentlemen, it is my great pleasure to introduce an individual whose honesty and sincerity are well-known, whose commitment to education is serious and wide-reaching, whose work in the field of linguistics has helped many students understand English better, whose wit and kindness make working together a pleasure. Ladies and Gentleman, I give you our English teacher, Rebecca Buckley.

- Make a dramatic introduction for one of your classmates, or a real person whose life and accomplishments you are familiar with.

Activity 7

Describe the qualities and characteristics of the ideal location for

a vacation
meeting new people
spending a rainy afternoon
retiring
raising a family

- Think of at least three statements for each category. (An ideal place for a vacation is a place where there is lots of sunshine.)
- Compare your descriptions to those of several other people.

Activity 8

Nicknames are often given to people to describe some physical characteristic or aspect of their personality. For example, someone with red hair is often called "Red." Someone with curly hair (or sometimes someone who is bald) is called "Curly." Someone whose nickname is "Sunny" is probably a cheerful, outgoing person.

- Here is a list of some other common American nicknames. Working with a partner, decide what characteristics would be likely for someone whose nickname is

Blondie	Cowboy	Muffin
Bubbles	Doc	Sport
Butch	Gramps	Tiger
Buster	Honey	Tubby

- Report your ideas to the rest of the class by using this kind of sentence: We think that someone whose nickname is_____ is probably a person who. . . .
- What else can you say about these nicknames? Are they used for children or adults? Could you apply them to both men and women? Do you think people would use these nicknames with people to their faces or behind their backs?
- Discuss how nicknames are used in other countries. Do you have a nickname? Why do people call you that name?

18

Special Problems in Using Present Time:

Temporary versus Permanent, Actions versus States

Task

Mary Rae is on a vacation in Florida, but she's not relaxing on the beach. She is participating in a program called Outward Bound. This program involves a lot of strenuous physical activity. People go to Outward Bound in order to challenge themselves and test their limits for physical and mental endurance. They come from ordinary jobs and spend two weeks in a wilderness environment hiking long distances, rowing many miles, and sleeping under the stars in primitive camps. The program is physically exhausting, but most people find it deeply satisfying as well. Many people say that Outward Bound has taught them things about themselves that they never knew. Most people are surprised to learn that they are much braver, stronger, and more capable than they originally thought.

Here is some information about Mary Rae and her life in New York, where she lives. There is also information about the things she is doing as part of her Outward Bound Program.

Mary Rae in New York	Mary Rae at Outward Bound
• Occupation: advertising account executive: visits clients, supervises a 25-person office	• Occupation: program participant: rows, hikes, climbs trees, builds fires, catches fish, picks wild fruit, cooks
• lives in a studio apartment	• sleeps in a tent, lives in a canoe
• often eats take-out Chinese food	• cooks all her own food, catches fish, and picks wild fruit
• worries a lot about her career	• doesn't think about her career at all
• doesn't get much exercise	• hikes or rows 12–14 hours each day
• doesn't spend much time outdoors	• doesn't spend any time indoors
• often has trouble falling asleep	• falls asleep almost instantly
• doesn't feel particularly challenged by her daily routine	• feels considerably challenged by each day's activities
• is somewhat bored with life	• is excited about growing stronger and more capable
• is not learning anything new	• is learning something new every day
• doesn't make new friends easily	• is making new friends easily

- What differences are there between the life she usually lives and the life she is living at Outward Bound? Write a paragraph comparing Mary Rae's normal life with her life at Outward Bound. Each sentence should contrast some aspect of her life in New York with her life in Florida. Here are some examples to get you started.

  Mary Rae normally spends her day as an account executive in a busy advertising firm, but here at Outward Bound she is spending 12 to 14 hours a day in vigorous physical activity. In New York, she supervises 25 employees, but here in Florida she is only supervising herself....

- Once you have written your paragraph, compare it to that of another member of the class. Did you use the same verb tenses to describe the activities, states, and situations in New York and Florida?

- Based on Mary Rae's experience, would you ever consider going to an Outward Bound Program? Why or why not?

Focus 1

Using the Present Time Frame in Generic Statements

USE

- We use the Present Time Frame most often to talk about general truths and relationships that are either true now or always true. Generic statements, conditional statements, and frequency adverbs are often used to indicate this generic meaning. This use of the Present Time Frame is extremely common in scientific and technical writing.

  (a) Supply **affects** demand in several ways. **If** supply exceeds demand, the cost of the commodity **generally decreases**.

  (b) **When** cost increases, demand often **drops.** Decreased demand **eventually results** in decreased supply.

Exercise 1

Here are reports of two scientific experiments. Change them into the Present Time Frame so that they serve as statements of general scientific principles, rather than as accounts of specific experiments.

EXAMPLE: *When baking soda is added to vinegar, a chemical reaction occurs. . . .*

EXPERIMENT 1:

(1)When baking soda was added to vinegar, a chemical reaction occurred. (2) The baking soda bubbled, and CO_2 was produced by the combination of elements. (3)When a candle was put next to the container while the chemical reaction was taking place, the flame on the candle went out.

EXPERIMENT 2:

(4)We wanted to determine whether weight affected the rate of acceleration of objects falling through space. (5)Two objects of similar size and shape, but substantially different weights— a cannonball and a volleyball—were dropped from the same height. (6)We found that both objects hit the ground at the same time. (7)This indicated that the acceleration due to gravity was constant.

Exercise 2

This is a case study illustrating the economic principle of supply and demand. A case study is an account of a specific situation. Rewrite this case study so that it becomes a general statement of basic economic principles and applies to more than this particular situation. You will need to change some of the specific references as well as the verb forms. Change *Kansas* to *rural areas,* change *wheat* to *commodities,* change *farmers* to *producers.*

(1)In Kansas, before the development of good interregional transportation, the price of wheat was determined by the relationship between its supply and the demand for it. (2)Supply was determined by how much wheat was available. (3)Demand was determined by how many people needed to buy it. (4)When the demand for wheat rose, the price also rose. (5)Farmers responded to the price increase by producing more wheat, since they could get a more profitable return on their investment of time and effort because of the higher prices. (6)With more wheat available, the competition to sell wheat also increased, and the prices of the wheat began to drop. (7)Fluctuations in wheat prices were extreme and continuous.

(8)But with the development of better interregional transportation, a more constant supply became available, since extra wheat could be brought in from other places. (9)Similarly, a more constant demand existed, since wheat could be sent to other areas of the country where harvests had not been as good.

Focus 2

Choosing Present Progressive or Simple Present Tense

USE

- When you use the Present Time Frame to talk about specific actions instead of general relationships or recurring events, it is necessary to make a basic distinction between things that are **true now** as opposed to things that are **always true.** Present progressive verb forms describe specific ongoing actions, and simple present verb forms describe things that are always true.

Recurring Activity, Habit, or Skill	Ongoing Activity Happening Now
(a) My friend **speaks** Spanish.	(b) He **is speaking** Spanish. He must be talking with Carlos.
(c) Bob **plays** the piano.	(d) Bob **is playing** the "Minuet in G" by Beethoven. It's so pretty!
(e) The children **sleep** in the upstairs bedroom	(f) Don't make too much noise. The children **are sleeping.**

Permanent Situation Extended Duration	Temporary Situation Limited Duration
(g) I **live** in Texas.	(h) **I'm living** with my uncle for the summer.
(i) Baking soda **works** well as a cleansing agent.	(j) The refrigerator **is working** well. I just had it repaired.

Exercise 3

Decide whether the verbs in these sentences refer to habits, skills, and recurring situations or to ongoing events. Choose the correct verb tense (**simple present** or **present progressive**) to indicate the difference in use. More than one answer may be correct, so be ready to explain why you chose the form you did.

1. Don't turn on the TV. I _____ (talk) to you!

2. My brother _____ (speak) a little Spanish. Let's ask him to help us with

   this letter from Mexico.

3. Janet _____ (study) for a biology midterm, so I don't think she can come

   to the party.

4. I _____ (leave) for work about 7:30 every morning.

5. Peter _____ (make) a big mess in the kitchen. You'd better go help him.

6. Gladstone _____ (do) his best, but he still can't run as fast as the others.

7. I _____ (try) to understand you, but you will have to speak more slowly.

8. Scientists _____ (discover) that many forms of mental illness are caused

    by chemical imbalances in the brain.

9. The traffic situation _____ (get) worse every year.

10. Learning a language _____ (get) easier when you practice outside of class.

Exercise 4

Decide whether these sentences talk about a permanent or temporary situation. Choose the correct verb tense (**simple present** or **present progressive**) to indicate the difference in meaning.

Bob (1) _____ (not take) a vacation this summer, because he (2) _____ (not

think) that he (3) _____ (have) enough money. He (4) _____ (teach) high

school chemistry, so he (5) _____ (get) three months of vacation, but teachers

(6) _____ (not make) much money. So he (7) _____ (look for) a temporary

job, since he can't afford to go anywhere. He (8) _____ (try) to find work as

a computer programmer. But most companies only (9) _____ (hire) workers on

a permanent basis. Bob (10) _____ (find) that it is difficult to locate short-term

employment. He (11) _____ (get) depressed about the prospects of three months

of nothing to do and nowhere to go. No matter how hard he (12) _____ (search),

he (13) _____ (begin) to realize that he may have to take a vacation, whether he

(14) _____ (want) one or not.

Exercise 5

Describe your daily routine. What activities do you do on a regular basis? Describe your typical day, starting from the time you wake up and ending with going to sleep at night. Write at least eight sentences about things you do on a regular basis.

Now describe three things that you are currently doing differently from normal, and why you have changed your routine. For example, "I'm living in a dormitory, because I have moved to a new city to go to school."

Focus 3

MEANING

Stative Verbs

 MEANING

- Stative verbs describe conditions or states. They do not usually take progressive form.
  (a) I **know** that you are unhappy right now.
  (b) NOT: **I am knowing** that you are unhappy right now.
- They fall into several general categories:

Sensory Perception	Mental Perception	Emotional Perception	Logical Relationship	
Appearance	**Knowledge and Belief**	**Feeling and Attitude**	**Cause and Effect**	**Measurement**
see hear feel appear look seem smell sound taste resemble look like	agree/ disagree with believe doubt feel (believe) imagine intend know recognize realize remember suppose think (believe) understand consider	love like hate dislike appreciate prefer want need mind	result in require depend on mean	weigh cost measure equal
			Possession	**Entailment**
			belong to possess have own owe	contain consist of include entail

Exercise 6

Work with a partner and ask him or her *Wh*-questions for the cues given. Your partner should give true answers, and then ask the same questions of you:

> **EXAMPLE:** which parent/resemble most
> *Which parent do you resemble most?*
> *I resemble my mother more than my father.*

1. what kind of fruit/taste best
2. what way/think/most effective to learn a foreign language
3. how/a sick person/appear
4. what/your notebook/contain
5. what/a handshake/mean
6. what activity/your parents appreciate/your doing
7. what/getting a BA degree/require
8. how many _____/you/own
9. who /that _____/belong to
10. what/not understand/American culture

Exercise 7

Report your partner's answers from Exercise 6 to the rest of the class.

> **EXAMPLE:** *Yoshiko resembles her mother more than her father.*

Focus 4

Verbs with Both Stative and Action Meanings

MEANING

- You can also use some stative verbs to describe actions. When you use them as action verbs, they usually appear in present progressive to distinguish their meaning from their stative uses. Here are some common examples:

Verb	Stative Meaning	Action Meaning
have	**(a)** I **have** three brothers. **(possess)**	**(b)** We're **having** a great time. **(experiencing)** **(c)** Mary's **having** a party next week. **(giving)**
mind	**(d)** I don't **mind** smoke. **(object to)**	**(e)** He's **minding** the children now. **(taking care of)**
see	**(f)** I **see** your point. **(understand)**	**(g)** John **is seeing** a specialist about his back. **(consulting)**
think	**(h)** I **think** you're right. **(opinion)**	**(i)** Be quiet! I'm **thinking**. **(mental activity)**
consider	**(j)** I **consider** money to be the root of all evil. **(opinion)**	**(k)** I'm **considering** going to Hawaii for vacation. **(mental activity)**
depends on	**(l)** Athletic ability **depends on** strength and practice. **(requires)**	**(m)** I'm **depending on** John to help me move next week. **(relying upon)**
be	**(n)** Jack **is** a teacher. **(identity)**	**(o)** Those children **are being** very noisy. **(behaving)**
feel	**(p)** I **feel** that you're the best choice. **(believe)**	**(q)** I'm **feeling** a little sick today. **(experiencing)**

- Other stative verbs can indicate the **act** of perception or measurement, or the perceptions or measurements themselves.

Verb	Perception/ Measurement	Act of Perception/ Measurement
smell	**(r)** The flowers **smell** wonderful.	**(s)** The dog **is smelling** the clothes of the missing boy.
taste	**(t)** That cake **tastes** delicious.	**(u)** Our host **is tasting** the soup to make sure it's not too salty.
weigh	**(v)** Joe **weighs** almost 100 kilos.	**(w)** The butcher **is weighing** that piece of meat.

Exercise 8

Decide whether these verbs express an action meaning or a stative meaning and indicate that meaning by writing the verb in **simple present** or **present progressive** tense in the blanks. In some cases, both answers may be correct, so prepare to explain why you chose the answer you did.

1. This cloth _____ (feel) really nice.

2. I _____ (consider) applying to go to Outward Bound.

3. Why did you ask that question? You _____ (be) really rude!

4. I _____ (believe) that Mary Rae _____ (have) a good experience at the Outward Bound program.

5. I don't like this beer. It _____ (taste) bitter to me.

6. I like people who _____ (mind) their own business and don't try to tell others what to do.

7. Bambang _____ (doubt) that he will be able to pass the TOEFL next week.

8. It _____ (look) as if we will get some rain later this week.

9. John _____ (feel) a little guilty about leaving Mary for so long. But I'm sure he'll get over it.

10. Learning a new language _____ (require) a lot of hard work.

11. These days the government _____ (require) people to take drug tests in order to get a government job.

12. Those children _____ (be) so naughty. I wish someone would make them stop teasing that poor kitten!

Focus 5

Other uses of the Present Time Frame

USE

- You can also use the Present Time Frame to
  - report actions as they are being performed. This use of the Present Time Frame is extremely common on radio and television shows that broadcast sporting events or "how-to" programs, such as cooking classes:
    - **(a)** Here's how we **make** cookies. First we **mix** a cup of flour and two eggs together in a bowl. Next, we **mix** in some sugar. A cup and a half **is** probably enough, but if we **want** sweeter cookies, we **add** at least 3 cups of sugar.
    - **(b)** Canseco **throws** the ball. Mays **hits** it. He **makes** a run to second base. He's **tagged** by Brown.
  - tell stories orally in more informal situations. This use of the Present Time Frame is most common with joke telling and stand-up comedians:

    One day I'm walking down the street. I see this guy talking on a pay phone. I know he's mad about something because I can hear him screaming all the way down the block. So, anyway, when I get up next to the pay phone, he stops shouting and asks me if I have an extra quarter. I tell him, "Sorry, man," and all of a sudden . . . .

Exercise 9

Tell this story aloud, as if you were Mary Rae describing her own experience. Recount it using the Present Time Frame to make it more vivid and less formal. The first two sentences have been done as an example.

> **EXAMPLE:** *There I am, standing in dirty swamp water as deep as my waist, but I'm having a wonderful time! The canoe we're rowing has gotten stuck on a log, so somebody has to get into the water and try to lift one end of it.*

There I was, standing in dirty swamp water as deep as my waist, but I was having a wonderful time! The canoe we were rowing had gotten stuck on a log, so somebody had to get into the water and try to lift one end of it. I looked into the water. It looked really dark and dirty. I knew there were a lot of poisonous snakes in this area. I knew there were also alligators. All of a sudden, I realized that I wasn't afraid of any of these things. I had complete confidence in my ability to free the canoe and to avoid getting eaten or bitten. Without another thought, I jumped into the water and started to pull at the canoe. At that moment, I knew that there was nothing that I was afraid to do, and nothing that I couldn't do if I put my mind to it. Outward Bound was one of the most important experiences of my life!

Activities

Activity 1

Give a demonstration on how to do something for the rest of the class. (This could be how to prepare a favorite food, how to perform some physical activity, or how to make some simple object.) Give verbal instructions at the same time that you demonstrate the activity.

Activity 2

Describe how your life has temporarily changed from its more normal routines. What things are you doing that you do not normally do? What things are you not doing now that you normally do? If you have moved to a new country recently, you may wish to compare your life in the new country with the old country. Otherwise, you can talk about any period when you have experienced a departure from your normal routines.

- Use the Present Time Frame to describe the differences. Think of at least five temporary changes in your activities. You may wish to use the statements you wrote in the Task as examples of the kind of statements you should make about yourself.

Activity 3

"How much does that cost?" "How much money do you earn?" "How much do you weigh?" "How old are you?" Most Americans consider these to be rude questions. They would not ask these questions of someone unless that person was a very good friend. In other cultures, people do not consider these to be rude questions, but they might hesitate to ask other kinds of questions, such as "How many daughters do you have?" "What do you do—what kind of job do you have?" or even "What kind of house do you live in?"

- Form a group and talk about what are considered to be rude questions in other cultures that you are familiar with. Present your findings to the rest of the class.

Activity 4

Describe some of the things that are happening in the picture that illustrates the Task at the beginning of this chapter.

Activity 5

We all learn our basic cultural values when we are very young. By the time we are adults, these lessons are so much a part of us that they are almost unconscious. A first step in learning about different cultures is learning to identify some of the deep basic cultural values.

- Write down at least five things your parents told you that were general truths when you were growing up. Make sure that the things you write are not orders or requests (My parents told me to clean my room), but rather, statements about things that are always true. (Good manners are important.)
- Compare your list to the lists of several other students. Are any of the statements the same on all your lists? Are there any interesting similarities or differences based on differences of cultures? What does this tell you about the values your parents tried to teach you?
- Report your ideas to the rest of the class.

19

Special Problems with Present Perfect Tense:
Describing Past Events in Relation to the Present

Task

North American Institute of International Studies
Application for Admissions

APPLYING FOR:

__ SPRING __ SUMMER __ FALL __ WINTER 19_____

DEGREE OBJECTIVE:

Undergraduate _____ Graduate _____
Major _____ Minor _____

PERSONAL DATA:

Name _____
Address _____
Telephone _____
Birthdate _____ Sex _____ Ethnic Background _____

EDUCATIONAL BACKGROUND:

List all secondary and postsecondary schools attended, including language programs.

Name and location of school   dates of attendance   degree granted   GPA

_____
_____
_____
_____

When American students apply to colleges and universities, they often have to write a personal essay about their individual character and achievements. Such essays often require students to identify ways in which they are different from other people who might also be applying for admission. The question asked on this application is typical. You may want to follow this suggested process in developing your answer:

- Identify a characteristic about yourself that might be of interest to the university admissions committee. It should be something that is related to your proposed field of study. For example, an applicant in international business may want to talk about his or her familiarity with and adaptability to other cultures; an applicant in fine arts may want to stress creativity, an applicant in science or technology may want to emphasize mathematical abilities.

- Next, identify at least one formative experience that helped you develop that characteristic.

- Finally, describe at least one achievement that this characteristic has enabled you to do. Here is an example:

  characteristic: I am adaptable.

  formative experience(s): I have lived in four foreign countries.

  resulting achievement(s):

  I have learned three foreign languages.

  I have lived comfortably in primitive conditions.

  I have seen things and experienced things that none of my friends has ever done.

  I have learned firsthand what life was probably like in earlier centuries.

- After you develop your list, compare it to that of another student in the class. You should work together to help each other explain and clarify your ideas.

- Once you have followed this process to organize your ideas, write your essay. Make sure you mention all the topics that were included in the question on the application form. Make sure your answer (1) identifies the characteristic, (2) identifies the experiences that have made you that way, and (3) mentions one or two things that you have been able to achieve as a result of that characteristic.

- If you wish, use Exercise 1 as an example of the kind of essay you should write.

Focus 1

Choosing Past Time Frame or Present Time Frame

USE

- When you describe past events in English, it is necessary to make a basic choice: whether to use the Past Time Frame or the Present Time Frame. In Unit 1, you learned that the moment of focus in the Present Time Frame is always NOW (the moment of speaking or writing). You also learned to use perfect aspect to describe sentences that are related to each other. Using the Past Time Frame instead of the Present Time Frame indicates that there is **no relationship** between the past event and NOW. This unit explores common situations where there is usually a relationship to NOW.
- You can use Past Time Frame to describe events that were fully completed in the past or occurred at a specified time in the past, but you must use the present perfect tense if those events continue to influence the present moment of focus in some way. Compare these sentences to see how a situation can determine whether to choose Past Time Frame or Present Time Frame:

Past Time	Present Time
(a) I **went** to Disneyworld three times while I was living in Florida. Now that I live in Ohio, it's too far away to visit.	**(b)** I **have gone** to Disneyworld three times, so I'm not really anxious to go again so soon after my last visit.
(c) I **worked** as a limousine driver during college. I **had** many opportunities to meet famous people.	**(d)** As a limousine driver, I **have had** many opportunities to meet famous people. It's one of the things I like about my job.
(e) I started that book, but I **didn't finish** it. It was too boring.	**(f)** I **haven't finished** that book yet. I've been reading it for several hours, and I hope to finish it soon.

Exercise 1

1) Underline all the verbs in the following passage. Mark verb phrases that refer to general truths or recurrent actions in Present Time Frame with (*a*). Mark verb phrases that refer to past events that have a relation to the present with (*b*). Mark verb phrases that simply refer to past events with (*c*). The first paragraph has been done for you as an example.

2) Why do you think the author changed from the Present Time Frame to the Past Time Frame in the second paragraph of her essay?

        (a)   *(a)*

(1)One of the characteristics that <u>makes</u> me different from many people I know <u>is</u> my adapt-

        (a)   *(a)*

ability. (2)I <u>am</u> flexible and comfortable in new or unusual situations. (3)I think this <u>is</u> because

    (b)   *(b)*

<u>I have had</u> a lot of experience living in foreign countries. (4)This <u>has given</u> me a lot of op-

portunities to face unfamiliar situations and to learn about unfamiliar customs and beliefs.

                                                   c

(5)My first experience in a foreign country <u>was</u> more than 20 years ago in Afghanistan.

     c   *c*

(6)I <u>taught</u> English in a small town in a rural area. (7)Life in my town <u>was</u> very simple.

               c

(8)Because there <u>was</u> no electricity and rather little contact with the outside world, my life

  c   *b*

<u>was</u> a lot like living in an earlier century. (9)I <u>have lived</u> in more modern situations since that

                               b   *b*

first experience, but everywhere I <u>have lived</u> it <u>has been</u> interesting and educational.

(10) As a result of my experiences in other countries, I have always been able to be comfortable with a simple life-style. (11) I have learned that relationships between people are very much the same, whether they have modern, busy lives, or old-fashioned, more peaceful lives. (12) I have learned to understand different ways of doing things and different ways of looking at the world. (13) Most of all, I have learned that *new* does not necessarily mean *better.* (14) This has made me adaptable, and this adaptability has helped me understand other people better.

Focus 2

USE

Relation to the Present: Still True versus No Longer True

USE

- One common way that past events relate to NOW is if they are still true. You can use present perfect to indicate that the situation being described is **still true.** You can use Past Time to talk about events that are **no longer true.**

Present Perfect Tense: (true now)	Past Tense: (not true now)
I **have worked** in a factory for three years. I **have been learning** how to operate complex machinery. I **have learned** how to operate three different kinds of machines so far. I still work at the factory.	I **worked** in an automobile factory for three years. I **was working** on the assembly line, but then they **promoted** me to foreman. I no longer work at the factory.

Exercise 2

Decide whether you should use the **past tense** or the **present perfect tense** for the verbs indicated in parentheses. More than one answer may be correct, so prepare to explain why you chose the form you did.

Bambang Soetomo (1) _came_ (come) to the United States last January to get a degree in mechanical engineering. Since he (2) _has been_ (be) in the United States, he (3) _has had_ (have) many new experiences. At home in Jakarta, servants (4) _cooked_ (cook) all his food. But here in the United States, Bambang (5) _has had_ (have) to prepare food for himself. In Indonesia, a lot of his university classes (6) _required_ (require) the ability to memorize large amounts of information. But here, Bambang (7) _has find_ (find) that memorization is not considered to be a very important skill in many of his classes. Of course, he (8) _was_ (be) ready for obvious differences in things like food and social customs, but he (9) _has not adjusted_ (not quite/adjust) to the subtle differences. He (10) _has learned_ (learn) that knowing about differences and dealing with them are two different things. In fact, he (11) _has been_ (be) rather homesick. In Jakarta, he (12) _had_ (have) a large group of friends, but here in the States, he (13) _has met_ (meet) only a few other Indonesian students, and none of them are in the same department he is. When he (14) _was_ (be) planning his trip to America, he (15) _planed_ (plan) to go home for a vacation after his sophomore year, but he (16) _changed_ (change) his mind since he (17) _got_ (get) here. He (18) _has spoke_ (speak) with his father about the possibility of coming home during his first summer vacation. His father (19) _hasn't decided_ (not decide) whether that's a good idea or not.

Focus 3

USE

Chronological Relationships: Until Now

USE

- Another way past events relate to the present moment is through a chronological (time) relationship. You can use present perfect to describe events or situations that began in the past and continue until the present. Common ideas that typically occur in this time frame are
  - the number of times something has happened:
    (a) Matt and Jeff **have seen** *The Wizard of Oz* over **a dozen times.**
    (b) I**'ve ridden** a roller coaster **once,** but I'll never do it again!
  - very recent events with *just:*
    (c) The doctor **has just left** the office. Maybe you can catch him if you hurry to the parking lot.
    (d) We**'ve just been talking about** your suggestions. Won't you join us?
  - sentences with *ever, never, since*:
    (e) I**'ve known** Stephanie **since** we **were** in high school.
    (f) I**'ve never eaten** snake meat. **Have you ever tried** it?

Exercise 3

Work with a partner. Take turns asking each other these questions. You can use the suggested topics or make up questions of your own.

1. Have you ever... (ridden a horse, been in love, seen a flying saucer...)? UFO
2. How many times have you... (eaten Chinese food, taken the TOEFL, driven a motorcycle...)?
3. Name three things you have never done but would like to do.
4. Name three things you have done that you don't particularly want to do again.

You should ask at least ten questions. Once you have collected the information, make a brief oral report about your partner to the rest of the class. The class should decide who has asked the most interesting or unusual questions.

Exercise 4

Do these sentences refer to situations that include the present moment or situations that are fully completed in the past? Indicate which by choosing the **past tense** or the **present perfect tense** for the verbs. More than one answer may be correct, so prepare to explain why you have chosen your answer.

My friend Bob is a very happy man. He just (1) _find_ (find out) that he (2) _has just won_ (win) a free trip to Hawaii. He (3) _has bought_ (buy) raffle tickets for years, but he never (4) _won_ (win) anything until six months ago, when he (5) _has won_ (win) an electric toaster. Since then, apparently, his luck (6) _has changed_ (change). He (7) _has gotten_ (get) more than a dozen prizes from various contests. Most of the prizes (8) _were_ (be) small, until last month, when he (9) _has won_ (win) a videocassette recorder and a color TV. I wonder if he (10) _has been thinking_ (think about) sharing his good fortune with his dear, kind friends.

Focus 4

Logical Relationships to the Present

USE

- Past events can also have a logical relationship to the present moment. The past event, although completed in the past, still continues to affect the present situation in some way. The logical connection can be a present result.
  - This present result can be stated explicitly:

Past Action	Present Result
(a) I have already seen that movie,	so I suggest we go see a different one.
(b) He has been wasting so much money	that I don't think we should give him anymore.
(c) I have always felt that beggars were lazy,	so I won't give this fellow any money.

256

- This result can be implied:

Past Action	Implied Present Result
(d) You **have spilled** ink all over my new tablecloth!	There's a mess.
(e) John **has obviously forgotten** about our meeting.	He is not at the meeting.

- The logical connection can also be the **speaker's or writer's attitude.** The event in some way is connected to the present in the speaker's mind. For example, reporters often introduce news stories with the present perfect tense to emphasize the connection with the present moment. Or a writer may mention a past event that has a connection to a point she or he is about to make.

Not Connected to the Present	Connected to the Present in the Speaker's Mind
(f) Did you find the article you were looking for?(a simple question)	**(g) Have you found** the article you were looking for? Because if not, I think I might know where you can find it.
(h) The White House **released** new figures **yesterday** concerning the balance of trade. (a simple fact)	**(i)** The White House **has released** new figures on the balance of trade in the last quarter. These figures **show** that imports continue to outstrip exports by more than 20 percent. (a news report)
(j) The historian Toynbee **once observed** that history repeats itself. (a simple fact)	**(k)** The historian Toynbee **has observed** that history repeats itself, and I believe that he is correct. (The writer is making a point.)

Exercise 5

Choose the sentence that reflects the most logical continuation of the ideas expressed in the first sentence. Both sentences are grammatically possible.

1. I **have told** you that I don't like the color green.
   (a) My brother didn't like that color either.
   (b) So why did you buy me a sweater in that color?
2. Jeff **met** Matt at a party.
   (a) They soon became the best of friends.
   (b) They share an apartment in San Francisco.
3. Bambang Soetomo **arrived** in America about eight months ago.
   (a) He has been adjusting to American life ever since.
   (b) He is living by himself in an apartment.
4. **I have been trying** to get in touch with my math professor since last week.
   (a) I didn't do well on the last exam.
   (b) Whenever I go there, she doesn't seem to be in her office.
5. Many historians **have noted** the parallels between the decline of Rome and the decline of the great nineteenth century colonial powers, such as Britain and France.
   (a) However, they have neglected to extend the parallel to the United States.
   (b) The purpose of this paper is to explore those parallels in relation to the United States, and its role in world economic development.
6. I **don't think** that Denise likes Peter very much.
   (a) Have you ever noticed the way she avoids looking at him when she speaks?
   (b) Did she say anything about her feelings to you at the meeting last week?

Exercise 6

Why do you think the speaker chose to use the present perfect tense instead of the simple past tense in these sentences? Is the relationship to the present a chronological one, a logical one, or a combination of both?

1. Scientists have discovered a number of interesting similarities between the atmosphere of Earth and that of Titan, one of the moons of Jupiter. They have found significant concentrations of water vapor, and other chemicals common to Earth. They hope to send another space probe to the planet within the coming decade.
2. If I have told you once, I've told you a hundred times: I hate broccoli!
3. Guess what? We've been invited to Liz's wedding. What should we get her for a gift?
4. Sociologists have often argued that easily available welfare payments to poor families do not significantly affect long-term poverty, but recent statistics show that this may not be true.
5. Shakespeare's reputation as a psychologist has grown in recent years. His plays have always reflected an uncanny understanding of human motivations.
6. Has Jill found a summer job? I was talking with my aunt, and she said her office might need a temporary computer programmer.

Focus 5

Present Perfect Progressive Tense

USE

- You can use the present perfect progressive tense to give additional information about events that have a relation to the present. Use the present perfect progressive instead of the present perfect to describe something that is
  - temporary rather than permanent:
    - **(a)** He **has been living** with his parents, but he hopes to move out now that he has found a job.
    - **(b)** He **has lived** with his parents since he dropped out of college.
  - a repeated rather than a single occurrence:
    - **(c)** I **have been thinking** about the problem, but I don't have a solution. Do you have any ideas?
    - **(d)** I **have thought** about the problem, and I have a solution.
  - continuous rather than repeated or recurring:
    - **(e)** It **has been snowing constantly** for the last three hours. I hope it stops soon!
    - **(f)** It **has snowed several times** since we got here, but there's still not enough snow for skiing.
  - uncompleted rather than completed:
    - **(g)** I **have been writing** my term paper. I still have to type it, proofread it, and staple it together.
    - **(h)** I **have written** my term paper. Let's go have a beer!
- Remember that stative verbs do not normally take progressive aspect even when they refer to states continuing until the present:
  - **(i)** Living in foreign countries **has required** a lot of flexibility.
  - **(j)** NOT: Living in foreign countries **has been requiring** a lot of flexibility.

259

Exercise 7

Choose the correct form, **present perfect** or **present perfect progressive,** to talk about these events. More than one answer may be correct.

1. I _____ (read) about the development of early forms of photography, and I _____ (learn) some very interesting facts about it. I would like to continue my research next semester.

2. That baby _____ (cry) constantly since we got here. I wish its parent would do something to make it be quiet.

3. Bob's brother _____ (resent) his winning that free trip to Hawaii ever since he heard the news.

4. I _____ (try) to explain that for the last 15 minutes. Aren't you listening?

5. I _____ (try) to explain that every way I know how. I give up!

6. I _____ (work) on this problem all afternoon. I think it's time for a break.

7. Rebecca _____ (expect) the police to call about the accident. That's why she wants to stay home this afternoon.

8. Bob _____ (tell) the office that he doesn't want to take a summer job until after returns from Hawaii.

9. The newspaper _____ (try) to contact Bob about some contest. They _____ (called) at least five or six times.

10. Bob _____ (dream) about visiting Hawaii ever since he read an article about volcanoes. He _____ (become) a real expert on them.

Exercise 8

Decide whether these passages should use the **simple present**, **present progressive**, **present perfect**, **present perfect progressive**, or **past tenses**. More than one answer may be correct, so prepare to explain why you made the choice you did.

PARAGRAPH 1

Bambang Soetomo (1) _____ (speak) English quite fluently. I wonder where he

(2) _____ (learn) it. He (3) _____ (study) mechanical engineering. He (4)

_____ (plan) to go to graduate school once he (5) _____ (get) his BS de-

gree. Bambang (6) _____ (live) by himself for the last few months. But he (7)

_____ (think) about getting a roommate. He (8) _____ (miss) his friends

back home a great deal, and this (9) _____ (affect) his studies. He (10) _____

(consider) asking his father for permission to come home during the summer, but he (11)

_____ (not do) so yet.

PARAGRAPH 2

Many historians (1) _____ (draw) a parallel between the decline of the Roman

Empire and more recent empires, such as Spain, Britain, and even the United States. Some

historians (2) _____ (argue) that such comparisons (3) _____ (be) not valid

because there (4) _____ (be) many variables that (5) _____ (affect) political or

economic development. For example, one of the biggest problems that the Roman Empire

(6) _____ (encountered) (7) _____ (be) transporting food to urban areas with

large populations. Technological advances (8) _____ (make) that particular problem

insignificant for today's modern "empires." Other historians (9) _____ (consider)

the parallel between ancient Rome and later empires invalid because they (10) _____

(feel) that today's empires (11) _____ (not consist) of political alliances, but rather

economic ones. The development of a global economy (12) _____ (change) the

way political powers (13) _____ (deal) with each other and with the people that

they (14) _____ (govern).

Activities

Activity 1

They say that everyone is an expert at something. Identify a special skill or ability that you have that enables you to do something better than most other people. Talk about the experiences you have had using that skill, and what you have learned from those experiences that would convince someone to give you a chance to use that expertise. Make a report to the rest of the class.

Activity 2

Bring in the front page of a daily newspaper and examine the articles with a partner or in a group. Find examples of sentences written in present time and past time. What tense are headlines generally written in? What tense are the introductory paragraphs generally written in? What tense is the body of the article generally written in? Can you find a pattern? Why do you think the author chose one time frame rather than another? Discuss your ideas with your partner or group, and present them to the rest of the class.

Activity 3

Experts in cross-cultural communication have found that most Americans tend to believe that most changes in life are usually good. This is not necessarily true in other cultures. Find out what important changes your classmates have made in their lives. Interview three other classmates. Ask them the following questions:

> Have you changed any habits or routines recently?
> Describe the changes.
> Why have you made the changes?
> How have the changes affected you?

Record your information on this chart:

Name	Description of Change	Reason for Change	Result of Change
Example	quit smoking	health concerns, price of cigarettes	stronger lungs, better energy, more money, more nervous, weight gain
1.			
2.			
3.			

- Based on the changes your group has experienced, decide whether you agree that changes in life are generally for the better. Present your group's ideas and reasons to the rest of the class.

Activity 4

American culture tends to value individualism, and, as a result, most Americans are taught from a very early age to look for ways that they are different from other people. Most Americans can easily identify a large number of personal experiences and characteristics that they feel make them different from other people.

- Interview three or four other people and ask them these questions:

  What experiences have you had that most other people have not?
  What things make you different from most other people?

  Record your information on this chart:

Student's Name and Nationality	Different Individual Experiences	Different Individual Characteristics
1.		
2.		
3.		
4.		

- Of the people you interviewed, who was able to think of the greatest number of individual differences?

Activity 5

You may wish to compare the responses of Americans and other students in your class to the questions you asked in Activity 4. Were the Americans able to think of more differences than your classmates? Were they able to think of these differences more readily? Were there other cultural groups that could answer these questions more or less readily? What do the similarities and differences tell you about cultural differences? Discuss these questions in a small group and summarize your ideas for the rest of the class.

UNIT

20

Special Problems with Future Time:
Using Present Tenses; Using *Will* versus *Going To*; Adverbial Clauses in Future Time

Task

Are you an optimist or a pessimist? Optimists generally look on the bright side of things. Pessimists tend to expect negative things to happen. What are your expectations about the future?

- Here are some current trends and issues. Share your knowledge about these issues with a small group of other students. Consider some of the issues and decide how they are likely to develop in the future.

    Positive trends: technological improvements, new medical treatments, longer life expectancy, better food crops, political changes, better communication, more rapid transportation, equal status for women, more education

    Negative trends: environmental problems (pollution, acid rain, global warming), population increase, new diseases, increased traffic, Third World debt, breakdown of traditional societies, declining resources

- Based on your discussion and your own ideas, consider the following question:

    Do you think that life 100 years from now will be better or worse than it is today? Why or why not?

- Write a brief paragraph expressing your opinions and your reasons for them. Begin your paragraph by stating whether you are optimistic or pessimistic about the future of the world.

Focus 1

Recognizing Future Time

FORM

- Some linguists say that English doesn't really have future tense, because
  - you can often use the simple present and the present progressive tenses to talk about events in the future:
    - **(a)** John **leaves** for Europe in three weeks.
    - **(b)** We' **re having** a test next Tuesday.
    - **(c)** When I **am** 50 years old, I will have a big party.
  - you can use modal forms for both the Future Time Frame and the Present Time Frame:
    - **(d)** **Will** you open the window **now**?
    - **(e)** There's someone at the door. It **should** be Peter.
    - **(f)** Denise isn't here **now**. She **must be** at the office.

It is important to recognize when these forms refer to future events and when they refer to events happening now.

Exercise 1

Do the verbs in the passages refer to future time or do they have some other function (e.g., present time, request, or recommendation)? Underline the verb phrases. Mark future time verb phrases with *(a)*. Mark present time verb phrases with *(b)*. Mark other meanings with *(c)* and describe the meaning. The first passage has been done for you as an example.

1. *(b)* (1)School always <u>begins</u> in September in the United States. (2)This coming year school
   (a) *(a)*
   <u>begins</u> on September 12. (3)Janet's <u>going to start</u> her third year of high school. (4)She's
   (a)
   <u>taking</u> chemistry, history, English, and advanced algebra. (5)She <u>might take</u> a theater
   (a)
   (c—ability)
   class, if she <u>can fit</u> it into her schedule.

2. (1)We're having a class picnic in just a couple of weeks. (2)As you know, school ends on

   June 15, and the picnic will be on the next day, so we're already making plans. (3)Most

   people are being really cooperative. (4)For example, Martha makes great potato salad,

   so she's bringing some to the picnic. (5)There should be enough for everyone to have some. (6)But George is being difficult. (7)He says he will come, but he won't bring anything. (8)Will you explain something to me? (9)Will you tell me why George is so stubborn? (10)He really should be more cooperative. (11)Everyone else is bringing something. (12)Why won't he?

3. (1)The next century should be an extremely important time in the development of the human race, (2)but the time for government action should be **now!** (3)If certain things don't begin to happen, the next century could be a very unpleasant period in the history of the world. (4)The population is increasing at an alarming rate. (5)In spite of this fact, the current government will not put additional funding into birth control research or family planning programs, either at home or overseas. (6)Supplies of fossil fuels (coal, oil, gas) are decreasing rapidly, but the government will not adequately support programs to develop alternative energy sources, such as solar power or wind-generated electricity. (7)The new century starts in less than a decade, (8)but it is the actions that are or are not being taken today that will determine whether the human condition will be better or worse than it is now.

Focus 2

USE

Present Tenses in Future Time Frame

USE

- You can use the simple present and present progressive tenses to describe future activities that are already scheduled or planned to take place in the future.
    - **(a)** Christmas **happens** on a Sunday next year.
    - **(b)** John's **leaving** for France in a week.
    - **(c)** Next year **is** Leap Year.
- You must mark future events that are not already scheduled with *will, be going to* or a modal of prediction. (*may, could, might,* etc.)
    - **(d)** We **will** go shopping if they have a big spring sale.
    - **(e)** I **am going to** travel to the Amazon someday.
    - **(f)** There **might** be a surprise quiz on Friday.

Exercise 2

Make at least five questions about things that will happen in this class at a future time that have already been scheduled. Ask your questions to another person in the class.

EXAMPLE: *What time do classes start next Tuesday?*
When are we having our next grammar test?

Focus 3

USE

Will versus *Be Going To*

USE

- *Will* and *be going to* both talk about future actions, but they have different uses.
- You can use *be going to*
  - to introduce a topic:
    - **(a)** **I'm going to paint** my apartment. First, **I'll** go to the store to get some paint. **I'll** also get brushes and rollers. I **might** paint the walls green, but I haven't decided yet.

      Subsequent sentences often use *will* or other modal forms.
  - to indicate a strong intention:
    - **(b)** I'm **going to go** to the party, whether you're there or not.

      Will can be used in such cases, but it is stressed in speech.
    - **(c)** I **will** go to the party, whether you're there or not.
  - to indicate definite situations in the immediate future:
    - **(d)** We shouldn't go hiking this afternoon. It's **going to rain** any minute!
- You can use *will*
  - for future actions that do not stress intention:
    - **(e)** John **will** study in France next year.
    - **(f)** I had better do it now, because **I'll be** busy next week.
  - for offers and requests in future time:
    - **(g)** I need some milk from the store. Oh, **I'll** get it for you.
    - **(h)** I've been invited to a party next weekend. **Will** you go with me?
  - to indicate refusal of an invitation or request:
    - **(i)** I asked him to help us, but he **will not do** it. (He has refused our request.)
    - **(j)** Denise **won't go** with us, no matter how much we ask her. (Denise has refused our invitation.)
  - to express general truths:
    - **(k)** Plants **will die** if they don't get enough water.
    - **(l)** Boys **will be** boys.
  - **(m)** A criminal **will always return** to the scene of the crime.

- When there is a possibility of interpreting a future action as a request, you should use **be going to** instead of **will** future actions.
    - **(n) Are you going to** buy a new car? (I know you were thinking about it. What have you decided to do?)
    - **(o)** AWKWARD: **Will** you buy a new car? (This sounds strange in English. It sounds like a request.)
- When the context makes clear that we are talking about a future action, not a request, either form can be used:
    - **(p)** Are you going to Mary's party?
    - **(q)** I don't know. **Will** John be there?
    - **(r)** I don't know. **Is** John **going to be** there?

Exercise 3

Decide which form, *will* or *be going to*, should be used in the following sentences. In some cases, both answers may be correct.

1. Charley (1) _____ (not go) to Rebecca's party. Gladys (2) _____ (be) there, and she and Charley don't get along anymore. She (3) _____ (probably drink) too much, and then she (4) _____ (want) to tell everyone about how they used to be engaged to be married.

2. I've got an extra ticket to the opera. (1) _____ (you go) with me? It (2) _____ (be) a great performance. Pavarotti (3) _____ (sing) the part of Falstaff. I'm sure he (4) _____ (be) wonderful.

3. I don't know what to do for my vacation. Maybe I (1) _____ (go) to Mexico. I know the plane ticket (2) _____ (be) expensive. Perhaps I (3) _____ (take) the bus to save some money. Your brother's taken the bus before, hasn't he? (4) _____ (you ask) him how the trip was?

4. Janet (1) _____ (finish) her assignment tonight, even if she has to stay up until dawn. It (2) _____ (not be) easy. She has to finish reading *War and Peace*, and then write a 10-page paper. She (3) _____ (probably be) up all night. Maybe her roommate (4) _____ (make) some coffee for her and do the dishes, so that Janet (5) _____ (not have) to worry about anything else.

5. Different plants need different amounts of water. Too much water (1) _____ (kill) certain kinds of plants. Other kinds require daily watering, and they (2) _____ (die) if they don't get it. Setting out a garden (3) _____ (require) some advanced planning to make sure that plants with similar water requirements (4) _____ (be) planted in the same areas.

Focus 4

MEANING

Other Modals in Future Time Frame

 MEANING

- You can use most one-word modals (**will, may, might, should,** and **could**) to make predictions about the **probability** of something happening in the future.

Form	Meaning	Use
will	**certain** 100% probability	**(a)** We **will** arrive in an hour.
should	**probable** 65%–80% probability	**(b)** Aunt Emily **should** like this movie.
may/may not	**quite possible** 35%–65% probability	**(c)** I **may** be a little late to the meeting.
might/might not *could*	**somewhat possible** 5%–35% probability	**(d)** Peter **might** not know the answer. **(e)** It **could** rain before we get there.
will not	**certain** 0% probability	**(f)** I **won't** be at the concert next week.

- *Shall* is not usually used in American English to talk about future actions or events. Using *shall* to talk about future actions sounds quite formal to the American listener. In American English, we use *shall*
  - to make offers:
    (g) Shall I peel you a grape?
    Should and *may* are often used in this context.
  - to suggest activities that both speaker and listener will participate in:
    (h) Shall we dance?
    (i) Shall we begin with the first exercise?
    Let's is a slightly more informal variant of this use.
- See Unit 21 for more information about and practice with predictions about future events.

Exercise 4

What are some likely developments in the areas listed below and what are your reasons for thinking so? Use a modal to indicate how likely your answer actually is.

EXAMPLE: What will life be like 100 years from now?

Life should be more complex 100 years from now, because of so many technological developments.

1. Will life be better or worse than it is today?
2. Will there be enough coal and oil?
3. Will there be a decrease in air pollution?
4. Will the overall climate grow warmer?
5. Will the rate of population growth be greater?
6. Will there be increased use of automobiles?
7. Will there be political stability?
8. Will there still be large differences between developing and developed countries?
9. Will there be cures for cancer, AIDS, and other diseases?
10. What will the "problems" be that people face in the twenty-first century?
11. Will there still be wars between countries?

Make up three questions of your own.

Focus 5

FORM

Future Time Frame Adverbial Clauses

FORM

- In the Future Time Frame, adverbial clauses always use present tenses.
  - **(a)** I'll do it tomorrow, **when I finish school**.
  - **(b)** NOT: I'll do it tomorrow, **when I will finish school**.
  - **(c)** I'm going to watch TV **as soon as I have finished my homework**.
  - **(d)** NOT: I'm going to watch TV as soon as **I will have finished my homework**.
  - **(e)** John is planning to have a party **while his parents are visiting relatives in Canada**.
  - **(f)** NOT: John's planning to have a party while his parents **will be visiting relatives in Canada**.

Exercise 5

Join the second sentence in each of these pairs to the first sentence using the suggested linking word. Make sure to change nouns to pronouns where necessary.

> **EXAMPLE:** I'll go to the movies. I will finish my homework. (after)
>
> *I'll go to the movies after I finish my homework.*

1. All my friends will be very relieved. The semester will end in a couple of weeks. (when)
2. I'm going to go to the movies every day. I will have finished all the household chores that have been postponed all semester. (once)
3. It will be almost three weeks after the last day of class. Janet will finally get her research paper completed. (by the time)
4. I'm going to read that book about magic. I'll have some time after the exams. (when)
5. Peter's going to spend every afternoon at the beach. The weather will be sunny. (while)
6. Matt and Jeff will be really tired. They are going to arrive in Phoenix by bicycle. (by the time)
7. Kevin and Libby are leaving for Europe. They'll finish their last exam. (as soon as)
8. Doug and Kathy are going to get married. They will be on vacation in Mexico. (while)
9. Even our teacher's going to take some time off. She will have finished grading the final papers and correcting the exams. (when)
10. The vacation will be over. We will realize that sad news. (before)

Focus 6

USE

Sequence of Tenses in Future Time Frame

USE

- Time relations between verbs in the Future Time Frame are expressed in the same way as verbs in the Present Time Frame or the Past Time Frame. You can indicate these relationships using
  - adverbial information:
    John will travel around Europe **before** he returns home.
  - aspect markers:
    John **will have visited** several other countries by the time he leaves for home.

Exercise 6

Read the following passage and underline each verb phrase. For each verb phrase, identify the time relationship between the verb and the moment of focus (100 years from today, the end of the twenty-first century). Does the verb happen **(a)at, (b)before, (c)during, or (d)before and during** the moment of focus? Mark it accordingly. The first two sentences have been done for you as an example.

(1)A hundred years from now <u>will be</u> *(a)* a wonderful time to be alive. (2)By the end of the twenty-first century, several basic changes <u>will have occurred</u> *(b)* in human society. (3)Most of the diseases that are common today will have been wiped out. (4)Scientists will have found cures for AIDS, Alzheimer's Disease, heart diseases, and cancer. (5)People will be living longer and healthier lives than they currently are. (6)People in developing countries will have been eating more nutritiously for several generations; (7)so, as a result, human beings will, on the whole, be larger, stronger, and more intelligent than they are today. (8)Scientists will have been researching ways to produce cheap, clean, nonpolluting energy. (9)So it is likely that by the end of the next century, there will be no smog, no acid rain, and no fears about global warming and the greenhouse effect. (10)Political changes will have removed the threat of nuclear war. (11)People will have been thinking in global terms for so long that it will no longer be necessary to have passports.

Activities

Activity 1

What day and time is it at this moment? Imagine what you will be doing **at this exact moment** 10 years from now, 20 years from now, and 50 years from now. Describe these activities to a partner or write a brief essay.

Activity 2

Who has the most interesting plans for the next vacation?

- Describe your plans to two or three other people. Listen to their plans. Once everyone has described his or her vacation, answer these questions as a group:

    Whose plans sound like the most fun? Why?
    The easiest to arrange? Why?
    The best opportunity to practice English?
    Decide on one more original category of your own.

- Report your decision and reasons to the rest of the class.

Activity 3

Choose one of these three questions and write a paragraph or make an oral presentation expressing your ideas.

- What major **political and economic changes** are going to take place in your lifetime? Describe them and explain why you think they are going to happen.
- What major **social changes** are going to take place in your lifetime? Describe them and explain why you think they are going to happen.
- What major **scientific advances** are going to take place in your lifetime? Describe them and explain why you think they are going to happen.

Organize a debate between optimists and pessimists. Using the Task at the beginning of this lesson, decide whether you are an optimist or a pessimist. Form groups of four or more. Be sure to have an equal number of optimists and pessimists in each group. As a group, choose one of the following areas of world affairs and discuss the current trends that are suggested here. Add one or two significant additional trends of your own. Optimists will then decide on reasons why they think the current trends will result in a better situation 100 years from now. Pessimists will decide on reasons why they think the current trends will result in a worse situation 100 years from now. Present both sets of predictions to the rest of the class.

Area of World Affairs	Some Current Trends
political developments	• wars between nations and within nations • political changes in specific countries
economic developments	• Third World debt • the balance of trade • the collapse of Communist economies • the growth in numbers of poor people in industrial societies
environmental developments	• global warming • the depletion of rain forests • the development of new energy sources
religious developments	• the growth of Islamic and Christian fundamentalism • the spread of Eastern religions (Hinduism and Buddhism) to Europe and North America
artistic and literary developments	• the spread of English as a world language • the impact of radio and TV on communication • the increasing importance of visual media (film, TV, photography) over print media (literature, newspapers)
scientific and technological development	• genetic engineering • new medical treatments • the growth of computers

21

Modals
of Prediction
and Inference

Task

Have you ever wanted to be a detective? Let's see how good you are at solving some puzzles. The following are three mysterious events. Discuss the possible causes with other students. Which causes are likely and which causes are not so likely? When nobody can think of any other possible explanations, turn to the Activities, read the additional clues, and try to solve the mysteries.

Mystery #1

A man lives on the 40th floor of a very tall building. Every day he rides the elevator down to the ground floor. When he comes home, he rides the elevator to the 20th floor, but he has to walk the rest of the way.
Why?

Mystery #2

In a room, a dead woman hangs by a rope, more than three feet above the floor. There are no windows, and the door has been locked from the inside. The room is empty: no furniture, no ladder. The only thing in the room is a single piece of paper.
What happened to the woman?

Mystery #3

A police officer receives an emergency phone call. There has been a terrible automobile accident, and a boy and his father have been badly injured and are both in critical condition. The officer has been called in to fill out the report and figure out what happened. The police officer arrives, takes one look at the boy and his father, and says, "You'll have to find someone else to deal with this. I'm too upset. This boy is my son!"
How can the boy have two fathers?

Do not look at the additional clues until you have thought of at least five possible explanations for each mystery.

Focus 1

Modals of Prediction Prerpositiedhie

MEANING

- Modals of prediction refer to the Future Time Frame. You can use them to indicate how likely or possible it is that some future event will occur.

Form	Meaning	Examples
will	certain	**(a)** We **will** arrive in one hour.
should	probable quite likely	**(b)** We **should** be able to get a good price for Andy's car.
may	quite possible possible	**(c)** I **may** be late tonight.
might **could**	somewhat possible	**(d)** You'd better take an umbrella. It **could/might** rain tonight.
may not **might not**	possibly not	**(e)** We **may/might not** get there in time.
shouldn't	probably impossible not likely	**(f)** This **shouldn't** hurt.
won't	impossible	**(g)** That **won't** happen.

Exercise 1

Make sentences from these cues using modals.

> **EXAMPLE:** certain: Andy/drive to New York for a vacation.
> *Andy will drive to New York for a vacation.*

1. probable: Andy/decide what to do about his car next week.
2. impossible: the car/work well enough for his trip to New York.
3. possible: Andy/get it repaired, if it can be done cheaply.
4. probably impossible: he/have trouble selling it.
5. quite likely: he/be able to get a good price.
6. possible: Andy's friend Paul/want to buy it.
7. possibly not: Andy/sell the car to Paul.
8. possibly not: the car/be in very good condition.
9. possible: Paul/expect a refund if he has troubles with the car.
10. certain: Andy/need the money to buy a plane ticket if he doesn't drive.

Exercise 2

Here are some activities. How likely is it that you will be doing these things next Saturday night at 8:00 P.M.?

doing English homework
watching TV
thinking about personal problems
going to church
reading a magazine

taking a bath
speaking another language
sleeping
writing letters to the family
having a good time with friends

Work with a partner. Ask questions with **will.** Answer questions with the appropriate modal of prediction. Prepared to report two or three of your partner's answers to the rest of the class.

EXAMPLES: *At 8:00 P.M. next Saturday, do you think you will be doing English homework?*
I won't be doing homework on a Saturday night. I might be at a disco.

Exercise 3

Write 12 true sentences about your plans for your next vacation, using modals of prediction:

two things that you will definitely do
two things that you will probably do
two things that you will possibly do
two things that you possibly won't do
two things that you probably won't do
two things that you definitely won't do

Exercise 4

Write 12 sentences about how you think life will be at the end of the next century, using modals of prediction:

two things that will definitely be true
two things that will probably be true
two things that will possibly be true
two things that possibly won't be true
two things that probably won't be true
two things that definitely won't be true

Focus 2

Modals of Inference   wniosek

- Modals of inference refer to the Present Time Frame. You can use them to describe logical conclusions about a current event or situation based on knowledge or evidence. Because they are statements of conclusion, you do not use these forms to ask questions.

Form	Meaning	Example
must	There is no other possible conclusion.	**(a)** That **must** be John. I've been expecting him.
should	This is a reasonable conclusion, but it is possible that there is another conclusion.	**(b)** John **should** be here somewhere. He said he was coming.
may/might/could	This is one of several possibilities.	**(c)** She **may** be unhappy. **(d)** They **might** have some problems. **(e)** John **could** be here.
may not/might not	This is one of several possibilities.	**(f)** She **may/might not** be here. I haven't seen her yet.
shouldn't	This is not a reasonable conclusion, but it could be possible.	**(g)** That **shouldn't** be Mary's brother. She told me he wasn't planning to be here.
must not	This is not a possible conclusion.	**(h)** I've looked everywhere for Mary. She **must not** be here.
can't/couldn't	This is impossible.	**(i)** That **can't** be John. I know he's still out of town. **(j)** He **couldn't** be in two places at the same time.

Exercise 5

Fill in the blanks with an appropriate modal of inference. There may be more than one correct answer, so prepare to explain why you chose the form you did.

1. There's someone at the door. That _must_ be my brother. I've been expecting him. But it _might_ be the mailman, or it _could_ even be a salesman.

2. Someone is ringing the doorbell. It _can't_ be my brother; he has a key. It _shouldn't_ be the mailman; he doesn't usually ring the bell. It _couldn't_ be a friend; all my friends think I'm still in New York. It _must_ be a salesman. Let's not answer it!.

3. I hope I can go to the movies with you tonight, but I _may not_ have enough money. I _should_ have enough, because I cashed a check yesterday. But I won't be 100 percent sure until I buy groceries and see how much money I have left. I really hope I can go. Everyone who has seen it says it's really good. It _must_ be very funny.

4. Martha looks pretty unhappy. She and George _must_ be having another one of their fights. I don't know what the problem is this time. It _might_ be because George is always working on his car. It _might_ be because Martha wants them to spend every weekend at her mother's house. It _couldn't_ be about money, though. That's the fight they had last week. They _must not_ have a very happy marriage.

5. Where have I put my wallet? It _must_ be somewhere! It _couldn't_ just disappear by itself. It _should_ be on my desk, since that's where I usually put it. But it _can_ be in my briefcase too. I sometimes forget to take it out when I get home.

6. Naomi _mustn't_ need money. She's always eager to pay when we go out for a night on the town. She never seems to have a job. It _must_ be nice to have enough money without having to work.

278

7. Frank _should_ have no trouble finding a job when he moves to California. It _could_ take a while, but I know he'll find a good position. He seems unhappy in New York. He _couldn't_ like living there very much.

Focus 3

Other Modal Meanings for *Will, Can,* and *Should*

MEANING
USE

- In the Present Time Frame it's easy to confuse the meaning of certain modals. **Can, will,** and **should** have other common meanings in the Present Time Frame that are easy to confuse with prediction and inference.
- You can also use **will** and **can** to make statements about the certainty or possibility of general truths in the Present Time Frame in addition to their use for predictions about the Future Time Frame.

General Possibility/Certainty	Specific Prediction
(a) My brother **can** be really grouchy when he first wakes up.	**(b)** He **might** be more cooperative after he has had breakfast.
(c) A criminal **will** always return to the scene of a crime.	**(d)** We **might** identify some suspects by watching to see who comes by.
(e) San Francisco **can** be cold and foggy in the summer.	**(f)** We **will** need our jackets if we go there.

- *Should* has two common uses in the Present Time Frame. You can use it to state a reasonable expectation or you can use it in hypothetical situations to imply that the opposite of what has been stated is actually true.

Reasonable Expectation	Negative Implication
(g) There's someone at the door. Oh, that **should** be my brother. He said he would drop by. **(h)** Is that Mary? Mary **shouldn't** be here. She had a date tonight.	**(i)** I **should** be happy that you're here. (I'm not happy.) **(j)** John **should** be here right now. (He's not here.) **(k)** I **shouldn't** be angry with you. (I'm angry.)

Exercise 6

Do these statements refer to a general truth, a specific prediction, or a statement of ability?

1. Babies will cry if they don't get fed.
2. Learning English can be quite rewarding.
3. Mrs. Smith can forget things if she's not careful.
4. I will be visiting your class.
5. People won't become fluent in a foreign language unless they practice.
6. Dogs won't eat vegetables.
7. Mary won't be very happy to hear the news about John's new "friend."
8. Mr. Merlin can do magic tricks.
9. Denise can be very difficult if she's in a bad mood.
10. Increased demand will always result in higher prices.

Exercise 7

Do these sentences express reasonable expectation or negative implication?

1. John should be pretty happy tonight. He just won $1,000. *res. exp.*
2. You shouldn't have any problems with the car. The mechanic has checked it over. *res. exp.*
3. Mary shouldn't be so disappointed about the test. Nobody else is. *negat. impl.*
4. I know the doctor should see you now, but he's still with another patient. *-//-*
5. I know Bob should be here any minute, because I just saw his car pulling into the driveway. *res. exp.*
6. You should be getting straight *A*'s in all your classes. What's the problem? *neg. impl.*

Focus 4

FORM

Phrasal Modals with Prediction and Inference

FORM

- You can use certain phrasal modals in statements of prediction or inference:

One-Word Modal	Phrasal Modal	Examples
will	be going to	**(a)** We're **going to** start the program a little late. It **will** begin at 8:20.
should	ought to	**(b)** Once the traffic starts moving, it **shouldn't** take too long. We **ought to** get there in about an hour.
must	have to/have got to	**(c)** That check **has to** be here someplace!

- You cannot use **ought to, have to,** and **have got to** to make negative inferences:

    (d) The test **shouldn't** be too hard.

    (e) AWKWARD: The test **ought not to** be too hard.

    (f) He **must not** care about his grade.

    (g) NOT: He **doesn't have to** care about his grade.

Exercise 8

Change the one-word modals in these sentences to phrasal modals if possible. (Not all the modals can be changed.)

EXAMPLE: I think it will snow a lot this weekend.

I think it's going to snow a lot this weekend.

You shouldn't find the exam difficult.

(Change to a phrasal modal is not possible because the statement is a negative inference.)

1. Traffic will get worse every year until we do something about the problem.
2. The traffic problem should begin to improve within ten years if we start making plans to solve it now.
3. It shouldn't be very difficult to find a parking place today, because it's Sunday.
4. Traffic is getting heavy; rush hour must be starting.
5. Jack must not have much money, because he drives a 15-year-old car.
6. The problem won't be solved by building more highways.
7. That will just increase the number of cars on the roads.
8. Traffic should flow more smoothly after they build the new tunnel.
9. This city must not have a very efficient public transportation system, because people seem to drive everywhere.
10. Commuters must be getting really tired of driving to work in such awful traffic.

Focus 5

Modals of Prediction and Inference in Past Time Frame

FORM
MEANING

- You can make predictions and inferences about things that happened in the Past Time Frame by using **perfect modals:**

Modal + *Have* + Past Participle
Alice **might have seen** that movie.

Modal	Present/Future Time	Past Time
must	**(a)** That **must be** John. I've been expecting him.	**(b)** That **must have been** John. I wasn't expecting anyone else.
should	**(c)** Peter **should be** here somewhere. He said he was coming.	**(d)** Let's ask Peter about the meeting. He **should have been** there.
may/might/could	Why is Martha crying? **(e)** She **may be** unhappy. **(f)** She **might be having** problems. **(g)** George **could be** the reason.	Why was Martha crying? **(h)** She **may have been** unhappy. **(i)** She **might have been having** problems. **(j)** George **could have been** the reason.
may not/might not	**(k)** She **may/might not be** here. I haven't seen her yet.	**(l)** She **may/might not have been** here. I didn't see her.
shouldn't	**(m)** That **shouldn't be** Mary's brother. She told me he wasn't in town.	**(n)** That **shouldn't have been** the reason.
must not	**(o)** I've looked everywhere for Mary. She **must not be** here.	**(p)** They didn't know what happened at the meeting. They **must not have been** there.
can't/couldn't	**(q)** That **can't/couldn't be** John. I know he's still out of town.	**(r)** I **can't have lost** it! **(s)** You **couldn't have forgotten** my name.

- In statements of prediction and inference, perfect modals indicate only Past Time Frame. For other modal uses, perfect modals indicate important changes in meaning. They are used for hypothetical statements, which are discussed in Unit 22.

   (t) Too bad you failed the test. You **should have** studied harder.

   (u) You **could have** helped me. Why didn't you?

Exercise 9

Change this passage to the Past Time Frame.

> **EXAMPLE:** Denise might not have enough time to finish the project today. That must be the reason why she isn't at the boss's birthday party.
>
> *Denise might not have had enough time to finish the project yesterday. That must have been the reason why she wasn't at the boss's birthday party.*

(1)Frank might be in California. (2)He should have no trouble finding a job. (3)It might take a while, but he has excellent qualifications and lots of experience. (4)He must be really unhappy in New York to want to move all the way across the country. (5)He must not like living in such a big city very much.

Exercise 10   Mom e

Write the appropriate perfect modal form in the blank. There may be more than one correct answer.

1. Someone called me up in the middle of the night. They hung up before I could answer the phone. It _must not have been_ (be) my brother; he doesn't have a telephone. It _might have been_ (be) someone I know, but why would they call in the middle of the night? It _must have been_ (be) a wrong number.

2. Where were you last night? I thought you were going to join us at the movies. You _must have had_ (have) enough money to go with us, because the tickets weren't that expensive. It's too bad you didn't come. I _may have been_ (be) able to lend you the money. And probably Peter _may have paid_ (pay) for your ticket. He's so generous. The movie was really funny. You _must have been_ (be) disappointed.

3. Janet looked really unhappy. She _must have failed_ (failed) another exam. I know she's already failed one midterm, and she had two more last week. It _may have been_ (be) her chemistry test. I know she was really nervous about it. It _may not have been_ (be) her calculus exam. She's really good at mathematics, and I know she studied a lot for it.

4. Bob looked everywhere for the missing documents. They _must not have disappeared_ (disappear) by themselves. He thought they _should have been_ (be) on the desk, where he usually put things he was working on, or they _should have_ (be) in his briefcase too. But when he looked, they weren't in either place. Then he remembered working on them at the office. He _must have left_ (leave) them there.

5. Who killed Judge Clarence? It _couldn't have been_ (be) his wife. She was in Switzerland learning how to ski. It _could have been_ (be) his accountant. Apparently there was some trouble with money. But nobody thought his accountant would do such a thing. There were a few clues. His wallet was missing. His brother's fingerprints were found on the candlestick that was used to kill the judge. The murderer _could have been_ (be) his brother. But Detective Nancy Mann was not convinced. It all seemed too simple. The brother was rich and didn't need the money. The murderer _must have been_ (be) someone else, someone who was actually trying to get the brother in trouble with the law.

Exercise 11

Use modals of prediction and inference to give possible reasons for these situations.

> **EXAMPLE:** The window was open. The TV was gone.
> *A thief must have broken into the apartment.*
> The students are quiet. They're listening carefully.
> *They might be taking a test.*
> *The teacher could be telling them about their final examination.*

1. Mary is crying. She's looking at a picture.
2. John's waiting at the airport. He's looking at his watch.
3. Rebecca was smiling. Her parents were congratulating her.
4. The men were digging holes. They were looking at an old map.
5. A woman was shouting happily. She had just received an envelope in the mail.
6. Bill studies every night. He sends applications to universities.
7. That man wears old clothes. He doesn't have enough to eat.
8. The firemen ran to the firetruck. They drove quickly to the house.

Activities

Task—Additional Clues:

- **Do not look at these** until you have thought of at least five possible explanations for each mystery.

  Mystery #1: The man is very, very short.

  Mystery #2: There's a big puddle of water in the room, and the paper is a delivery bill from an ice company.

  Mystery #3: The police officer is a woman.

Activity 1

Watch a television program (comedy or drama–not a news show or program with a narrator) for a few minutes without turning on the sound. You should be able to see, but not to hear, what's going on. Describe at least ten interactions between characters. Describe exactly what happened, your interpretation of what happened, and your reasons for thinking so.

Description of what happened	**Interpretation of the action**	**Reason for your interpretation**
Who did what?	What was the character's reason or purpose?	Why do you think so?

- Then write a paragraph that describes what you saw and what you think was happening. Be sure to distinguish between things that might have been going on versus things that must have been going on. Be sure to give reasons for all of your interpretations.
- Your teacher may want you all to watch the same program so that you can compare your interpretations with those of other students in the class.

Activity 2

Do you have friends or family living in another country? What time is it at this moment in that country? (How many hours' difference is there between that country and where you are now?) Taking the time difference into account, talk or write about what you think they are doing at this very moment.

Activity 3

These are pictures of six household items that are no longer used today. The size of each object has been indicated. Can you tell what function these objects had by looking at their form?

9"   48"   10¼" × 6⅝"

30" sq.   12"   12" long

- Work with a partner and discuss what you think each object might have been used for. Explain what its function might have been, and your reasons for thinking so.
- Compare your ideas to those of other students in the class. After you have presented your ideas to the class, your teacher will tell you what the actual use of each of the objects was.

Activity 4

Do you know how to predict someone's future by looking at his or her palm? Here is a diagram of some of the important lines of the palm. If the line is deep and strong, the person should have favorable developments in those areas. If the line is weak or broken, this indicates that the person may have trouble in that area. Using this reference guide, choose a partner, examine his or her palm, and make predictions about his or her future.

U N I T

22

Hypothetical Statements

Task

What things about your life would you change if you had the chance? Nadine Stair, from Louisville, Kentucky, wrote the following essay at the age of 85.

IF I HAD MY LIFE TO LIVE OVER

I'd dare to make more mistakes next time. I'd relax. I would <u>limber</u> up. I would be <u>sillier</u> than I *foolish* have been this trip. I would take fewer things seriously. I would take more chances. I would take more trips. I would climb more mountains and swim more rivers. I would eat more ice cream and less beans. I would perhaps have more actual troubles, but I'd have fewer imaginary ones.

You see, I'm one of those people who live sensibly and/sanely hour after hour, day after day. Oh, *practically impossible* I've had my <u>moments</u>, and if I had it to do over again, I'd try to have nothing else. Just moments, one after another, instead of living so many years ahead of each day. I've been one of those persons who <u>never goes anywhere</u> without a thermometer, a hot water bottle, a raincoat, and a parachute. If I had to do it again, I would travel lighter than I have.

If I had my life to live over, I would start barefoot earlier in the spring and stay that way later in the fall. I would go to more dances. I would ride more <u>merry-go-rounds</u>. I would pick more daisies.

- First, discuss this essay with a partner. What is Nadine Stair's philosophy of life? Do you agree or disagree with her attitude about what things are important? Do you think that she is speaking literally about swimming rivers, climbing mountains, and carrying a parachute, or do you think these are metaphorical examples of her attitude toward life? What does she mean by "moments"? You and your partner should summarize this essay in one or two sentences. Compare your ideas with those of the rest of the class.

- Next, decide how you would live your life differently if you could. Make a list of things that you are dissatisfied with, or things that you wish you could change. Once you have made your list, write how you would do it differently. Here are some examples:

DISSATISFACTIONS	**HOW MY "IDEAL" LIFE WOULD BE DIFFERENT**
• I don't have enough money.	• I would have lots of money.
• I have to spend too much time studying.	• I wouldn't have to spend a lot of time studying.
• I don't like living in a place with cold winters.	• I would live in a place that was warm all the time. (Or: I wouldn't live in a place that has cold winters.)
• Some people don't like me.	• Everyone would like me.

• Finally, use your list of the things you would or would not do to write a brief essay like Nadine Stair's. Write a paragraph on how you would live your life differently than you are currently doing, and what things you would change if you could.

Focus 1

Hypothetical Meaning

MEANING

English makes a grammatical distinction between real situations, or **actual situations**, and **hypothetical situations**. Hypothetical situations are very common in both spoken and written English. You can use them

• to talk about things that are not true or are impossible.
• to imply that the opposite situation is actually true.
• to be more polite.

It is important to recognize hypothetical statements and to understand the implied meaning of these kinds of statements.

Hypothetical Statement	Implied Meaning
(a) If I had a million dollars, I would buy a nice house.	I don't have a million dollars, so I probably won't be able to buy a nice house.
(b) If we were in Hawaii right now, we wouldn't have to be studying grammar. We could be lying on the beach.	We're not in Hawaii; we're in English class. We can't lie on the beach because we're studying grammar.
(c) You should be happy with your life. Many people would love to have half the opportunities that you do. If I were you, I wouldn't feel so sorry for myself, and I would count my blessings!	You aren't happy with your life. Many people don't have even half the opportunities that you have. I am not you, but I think you feel sorry for yourself, and you don't count your blessings.
(d) I wish we weren't in school. If we weren't in school, we could be almost anywhere. We could be at the beach or at the movies. We could be relaxing or having fun. We wouldn't have to be studying English. Wouldn't that be interesting?	It's too bad we're in school. If you're in school, you can't be anyplace else. You can't be at the beach or at the movies. You can't be relaxing or having fun. You have to be studying English. Isn't that boring?

Exercise 1

Here are some other examples of hypothetical statements. Choose the sentence that correctly reflects their implied meaning:

1. If you had done your homework, you would have gotten an *A*.
   - **(a)** You didn't get an *A* because you didn't do your homework.
   - **(b)** You did your homework, and so you got an *A*.
2. You could have brought a friend to the party.
   - **(a)** You had permission, but you came alone.
   - **(b)** You were able to bring a friend.
3. You could have been more careful with your homework.
   - **(a)** You had the ability to do good work.
   - **(b)** You were careless with your homework.
4. You should have seen the doctor before you got so sick.
   - **(a)** You followed my advice.
   - **(b)** You did not follow my advice.
5. You might at least have cleaned the house before my mother got here!
   - **(a)** It was still dirty when she arrived.
   - **(b)** It is possible that you did it.
6. I would have been here early, but the traffic was terrible!
   - **(a)** I arrived early.
   - **(b)** I arrived late.
7. I wish you had come to the lake last weekend.
   - **(a)** You did not come.
   - **(b)** You were there.
8. Let's pretend that we had a new president.
   - **(a)** We do not have a new president.
   - **(b)** We have a new president.

290

Exercise 2

For these hypothetical statements in Nadine Stair's essay, write a nonhypothetical sentence describing the condition that was actually the case. The first few have been done for you:

Hypothetical Statement	Implied Meaning
1. I'd dare to make more mistakes next time.	**1.** I was afraid of making mistakes.
2. I would be sillier than I have been this trip.	**2.** I wasn't silly enough.
3. I would take fewer things seriously.	**3.** I took too many things seriously.
4. I would take more trips.	**4.** I didn't take many trips.
5. I would eat more ice cream and less beans.	**5.** I ate less ice cream and more beans.
6. I would perhaps have more actual troubles, but fewer imaginary ones.	**6.** I didn't have imaginary worried too much?
7. I would travel lighter than I have.	**7.** I didn't travel much lighter cup
8. I would start barefoot earlier in the spring.	**8.** I didn't
9. I would go to more dances.	**9.** I didn't have much fun.
10. I would ride more merry-go-rounds.	**10.** I didn't – ir
11. I would pick more daisies.	**11.** I didn't pick up many daisies

Exercise 3

There are three nonhypothetical statements in Nadie Stair's essay. What are the sentences that describe her actual life and character, rather than the life she wishes that she had?

Exercise 4

Are these sentences hypothetical statements or inferences about actual events? If they are hypothetical statements, restate the implied meaning.

EXAMPLES: Those two are always together, so if she attended the meeting, he did too.

inference about a real event

If the weather hadn't been so cold yesterday, the picnic would have been a lot more fun.

hypothetical statement. The weather was cold yesterday, so the picnic wasn't much fun.

1. I would come to your party if I didn't have to work.
2. If John went to Hawaii on vacation, he must have spent a lot of money.
3. If Bill could afford to retire, I'm sure he would have done so by now.
4. I wouldn't tease that dog if I were you.
5. Suppose you had your own private jet. Where would you go for the weekend?
6. If Bill left when he had planned, he should be here any minute.
7. If my brother needed money, he always asked to borrow it from me.
8. Suppose I cook a big casserole for the party. Do you think there would be enough food?

Focus 2

Hypothetical Conditionals

MEANING

We often phrase hypothetical statements in terms of conditions and results. Compare these nonhypothetical conditionals (see Unit 15) with their hypothetical counterparts. Notice the important differences in implied meaning.

Factual, Predictive, or Inferential Conditionals	Implied Meaning
(a) If I **have** the time, I always **clean** the kitchen before I go to work.	I always do this whenever I have time.
(b) If I **don't have to work, I will come** to your party.	I don't know if I can come, because there's a chance that I may have to work.
(c) If Mary **was** at the lecture yesterday, I'm sure she **took** very complete notes.	Maybe she was there and took notes.

Hypothetical Conditional	Implied Meaning
(d) If I **had** the time, **I would clean** the kitchen before leaving for work.	I don't do it, because I don't have time.
(e) If I **didn't have to work, I would** come to your party.	I can't come, because I have to work.
(f) If Mary **had been** at the lecture, I'm sure she **would have taken** very complete notes.	She wasn't there, so she didn't take notes.

Exercise 5

Match these statements with their correct implied meaning.

Statement	Implied Meaning
1. (a) If John has the money, he always stops for a cup of espresso on his way to class. **(b)** If John had the money, he would always stop for a cup of espresso on his way to class.	**(a)** He doesn't usually do this, because he usually doesn't have the money. **(b)** He always does this whenever he has the money.
2. (a) If I had to work, I wouldn't be helping you with your homework. **(b)** If I have to work, I won't be able to help you with your homework.	**(a)** I may have to work. **(b)** I don't have to work.
3. (a) If Bambang took the TOEFL yesterday, I'm sure he did very well. **(b)** If Bambang had taken the TOEFL, I'm sure he would have done very well.	**(a)** Bambang didn't take the TOEFL. **(b)** Maybe Bambang took the TOEFL.

Focus 3

FORM

Hypothetical Statements in Present and Future Time Frames

FORM

You can use past tense forms to indicate that all these statements of condition and result are hypothetical and, therefore, not possible.

Past Tense Verb Forms Refer To	*Would/Could/Might* + Verb Refer To
Present Conditions	**Present/Future Results**
(a) If I **had** time,	I **would clean** the kitchen before leaving for work.
(b) If I **didn't have to work**,	I **would come** to your party.
(c) If I **were** rich,	I **would give** you a million dollars.
(d) If I **could speak** English,	I **wouldn't need** to read this unit.
Future Conditions	**Present Results**
(e) If we **didn't have to go** to school tomorrow,	we **could stay up** all night tonight.
(f) If John **weren't going to spend** next year in France,	Mary **might not be** so annoyed with him now.
	Future Results
(g) If I **graduated** next semester, **(h)** If I **were to graduate** one semester earlier,	it **would be** easier to find a job. it **would be** easier to get a teaching job right away.

These structures are an indication of hypothetical statements:

- *If*-clauses use *were* for singular subjects, rather than *was*, in most written and formal spoken English.
    - **(i)** If my mother **were** here, she would want us all to wash our hands.
    - **(j)** If Mary **were** coming to the party, she could bring the potato salad.
- Future hypothetical conditions are stated with past tense forms or *were to*. *Were to* is more common in formal English, and indicates that the possibility is very unlikely.
    - **(k)** If you **passed** TOEFL **next month**, you could probably begin academic studies next semester.
    - **(l)** I don't think you'll pass the TOEFL next month, but if you **were to do so**, we could have a party to celebrate.

Exercise 6

Change these statements of condition and result into hypothetical conditionals.

EXAMPLE: (Condition) I'm not the teacher of this class.
(Result) We have too much homework.
Hypothetical: If I were the teacher of this class, we wouldn't have so much homework.

1. I don't have a million dollars. I can't afford to buy you a new car.
2. I don't yet speak English perfectly. I still have to study grammar.
3. Doctors have to spend so many years in medical school. Medical care is quite expensive.
4. My mother doesn't know how I am living now. She's not worried about me.
5. I am not President of my country. I don't have much influence on world events.
6. I have many good friends. My life is busy and rewarding.
7. The TOEFL is a difficult examination. Many people can't pass it on the first try.
8. There are too many irregular verbs in English. It isn't an easy language to learn.
9. There aren't enough places in universities in other countries. Many students come to the United States for university study.
10. The weather reporter has forecast heavy rains for the entire day tomorrow. We won't have the picnic.

Exercise 7

Here are some hypothetical conditions. Add hypothetical results that are true for you:

EXAMPLE: If I could be anywhere in the world at this moment, . . .
I would be home in bed.

1. If I were going to attend any American university tomorrow, ...
2. If I were President of the United States, ...
3. If my mother knew how I was living now, ...

4. If I were the teacher of this class, ...
5. If I didn't have to worry about the TOEFL, ...
6. If I were to go home next week, ...
7. If I had all the money I needed, ...
8. If I were the same age as my parents, ...

Exercise 8

Here are some hypothetical results. Add hypothetical conditions that are true for you.

EXAMPLE: I would take a vacation . . .
if I didn't have to pass the TOEFL.

1. I wouldn't need to work . . . .
2. I would bring my family here for a visit . . . .
3. We wouldn't come to school . . . .
4. We wouldn't need umbrellas . . . .
5. I wouldn't be studying English . . . .
6. I wouldn't have to take the TOEFL . . . .
7. The world would be a much better place . . . .
8. I would give my grammar teacher $1,000 . . . .

Exercise 9

Compare your answers to Exercise 7 and 8 with those of another student. Report some of his or her responses to the rest of the class:

EXAMPLE: *May says that if she were the teacher of this class, she would give me an A.*

Focus 4

Hypothetical Statements in Past Time Frame

FORM

You can use past perfect forms and past modals with *have* + **past participle** to indicate hypothetical situations in the Past Time Frame.

Past Perfect Verb Forms Refer to	*Would Have/Could Have/Might Have/ Should Have* + **verb** Refer to
Past Hypothetical Conditions	**Past Hypothetical Results**
(a) If Mary **had been** at the lecture,	I'm sure she **would have taken** very complete notes. She **wouldn't have minded** sharing them. She **would have let** you borrow them.
	Would/Could/Might + **verb** Refer to
	Present or Future Results
(b) If William the Conqueror **hadn't invaded** England in 1066, **(c)** If I **had been born** in the last century, **(d)** If we **hadn't saved** enough money last year,	the English language **would probably have** a lot fewer words of French origin. I surely **wouldn't be** alive today. we **wouldn't be able to take** a vacation next summer.

Focus 5

Inverted or Question Word Order for Hypothetical Conditionals

USE

In formal written English, you can indicate hypothetical conditions in clauses with a *were* or *had* auxiliary by omitting the *if* and using question word order. This is not very common in spoken English.

Inverted Form	Regular Form
(a) Had I known that you were coming so late, I wouldn't have waited.	**(b) If I had known** that you were coming so late, I wouldn't have waited.
(c) Were I in charge of this business, I would make some big changes.	**(d) If I were** in charge of this business I would make some big changes.

Exercise 10

Change these nonhypothetical statements of condition and result to hypothetical conditionals.

> **EXAMPLE:** I wasn't alive 100 years ago. I have been able to fly all over the world.
>
> *If I had been alive 100 years ago, I wouldn't have been able to fly all over the world.*

1. My parents didn't speak English when I was a baby. I have to learn it in school.
2. English became a language of international business after World War II. Most developing countries require students to study it in high school.
3. Modern English developed from several different languages: French, German, Latin, Dutch, and even Norwegian. As a result, the grammar and spelling rules are very irregular.
4. England was invaded by France in 1066. Many French words replaced the traditional Anglo-Saxon ones.

Exercise 11

Here are some past conditions.
   Add past-time hypothetical results that are true for you.

> **EXAMPLE:** If I had been born 100 years ago...
>
> *I wouldn't have had a chance to travel.*

1. If my parents had spoken English when I was a baby....
2. If America hadn't won World War II....
3. If the grammar of English hadn't developed from so many different languages....
4. If advanced computer technology hadn't been developed in the United States....
5. If I had never studied English....

Add present or future time results to these sentences:

> **EXAMPLES:** If I had been born 100 years ago...
>
> *I probably wouldn't be alive today.*
>
> *my great grandchildren might be entering the university in the next few years.*

6. If I had been born in this country....
7. If the Japanese had won World War II....
8. If my parents hadn't wanted me to learn English....
9. If computers hadn't become so inexpensive and widely available....
10. If I had already gotten a score of 650 on the TOEFL....

Exercise 12

The following are hypothetical results. Add appropriate past-time conditions.

EXAMPLE: I wouldn't have had a chance to travel...
if I had been born 100 years ago.

1. I wouldn't have asked you to join us....
2. I would not be studying English now....
3. English grammar would be much more regular....
4. Fax machines wouldn't be so popular in Asian countries....
5. America wouldn't be spending so much money on military expenditures....
6. Transoceanic telephone calls wouldn't be possible....
7. There wouldn't have been such sweeping political changes in Eastern European countries....
8. Modern antibiotics might not have been discovered....
9. Life today would be much more difficult....
10. I wouldn't have to answer this question....

Exercise 13

Compare your answers in Exercises 11 and 12 with those of another student. Report some of his or her responses to the rest of the class:

EXAMPLE: *May says that if she had been born 100 years ago, she wouldn't have been able to study medicine.*

Exercise 14

From the sentences you made in Exercises 7, 8, 11, and 12, write new sentences in non-hypothetical language.

EXAMPLES: If I had a million dollars, I would give you a new car.
I don't have enough money to give you a car.

I would take a vacation, if I didn't have to finish this project.
I have to finish this project, so I can't take a vacation.
I can't take a vacation because I have to finish this project.

I wouldn't have asked you to join us if I had known you were going to be so rude.
I asked you to come because I thought you would be more polite.

If I had been born 100 years ago, I wouldn't have had a chance to travel widely.
A hundred years ago people like me didn't have a chance to travel widely.

Exercise 15

These passages contain hypothetical statements.

- Underline the hypothetical statements.
- Rewrite the sentences using nonhypothetical language. Be sure that your restatements reflect the actual time and preserve the actual meaning. The first paragraph of the first passage has been done for you as an example.

> **EXAMPLE:** (2) *Governments spend too much on arms, so not enough money is available for economic development, education, and health care.*

1. (1)Some students of international relations feel that individual governments shouldn't be spending so much money on military expenditures. (2)<u>If governments stopped spending so much on arms, more money would be available for economic development, education, and health care.</u>

     (3)Everyone agrees that some kind military force is necessary to maintain global stability, but these experts feel that it could be some sort of multinational peacekeeping force, administered by the United Nations. (4)If countries formed joint regional defense programs, one or two "superpowers" would be less likely to see themselves as responsible for maintaining global stability.

     (5)Pacifists point out that if the size of military forces were reduced—or even eliminated—then that money would be available for nonmilitary purposes. (6)This would enable governments to give more support to social programs. (7)Better social programs would improve social conditions. (8)Improved social conditions worldwide would reduce the need for wars even more.

2. (1)Many important developments in science have happened by accident. (2)Discoveries have often been made because someone was in the right place at the right time, or because someone made a mistake and got an unexpected result. (3)For example, if Sir Isaac Newton hadn't decided to take a nap under an apple tree, he wouldn't have been hit on the head by a falling apple. (4)It was this event that inspired him to formulate the Law of Gravity. (5)If Sir Alexander Fleming hadn't left his sandwich sitting on a laboratory windowsill and forgotten about it, he would not have discovered the mold that contains penicillin. (6)That's how he first found out about the antibiotic properties of certain fungi. (7)Had Christopher Columbus correctly calculated the actual size of the earth, he would never have tried to reach Asia by sailing west. (8)If that hadn't happened, the European discovery of the New World might have occurred in 1592, instead of 1492.

3. (1)The commercial development of the fax machine (which enables a person to send a photocopy of a document via telephone) has literally exploded in a phenomenally short period of time. (2)But its use wouldn't have grown as rapidly as it has, had certain Asian writing systems been able to adapt well to other forms of transmission. (3)If the writing systems of Chinese and Japanese were not so complex, people would be able to use other means (such as telegraph or digital computer display) to communicate information over long distances.

(4)Western languages use only 20 to 30 symbols to communicate ideas, so each individual letter can be easily translated into a specific series of electronic impulses. (5)Electronic digital transmission of western languages has been possible ever since the invention of the telegraph, nearly 150 years ago. (6)If Western languages used a writing system like that of Chinese, such digital transmission would probably never have been developed. (7)Chinese requires 3,000 to 5,000 different individual characters to communicate ordinary day-to-day events and ideas. (8)This makes digital transmission impractical. (9)If there weren't so many individual characters, or if the writing system had a clear correlation between a single symbol and a single sound, the fax would surely not have become so widely used in such a short period of time.

(10)In the last five years, fax machines have virtually replaced other communications systems, especially in Asia. (11)It is simply easier to write a character and transmit the image than it is to try to invent some system that "translates" a visually complex symbol into a series of electrical impulses. (12)Had this not been the case, the widespread use of fax machines would probably not have happened so quickly.

Focus 6

Mixing Hypothetical and Actual Statements

USE

- You can sometimes mix actual conditions and hypothetical results in a single statement.

Actual Condition	Hypothetical Result
(a) I had to work last night.	(b) **Otherwise** I would have come to your party.
(c) Peter brought a doctor's excuse to explain his absence.	(d) **Otherwise** Denise would have accused him of being irresponsible.
(e) It's going to rain tomorrow.	(f) **Otherwise** we could have the luncheon outside.

Hypothetical Result	Actual Condition
(g) I would have come to your party last night,	**but** I had to work.
(h) Denise would have accused Peter of being irresponsible,	**but** he brought a doctor's excuse to explain his absence.
(i) We could have the luncheon outside,	**but** it's going to rain.

Exercise 16

The following are some actual conditions. State a hypothetical result by using *otherwise* or *but*.

EXAMPLE: I'm not rich.

I'm not rich. Otherwise I would loan you the money you asked for.

I would loan you the money you asked for, but I'm not rich.

1. I don't have a million dollars.
2. I don't yet speak English perfectly.
3. Doctors have to spend many years in medical school.
4. My mother doesn't know how I am living now.
5. My father is not the leader of my country.
6. I have many good friends.
7. The TOEFL is a difficult examination.
8. English isn't an easy language to learn.
9. Many students come to the United States for university study.
10. The weather forecaster has predicted heavy rain for tomorrow afternoon.

Focus 7

USE

Using Hypothetical Statements

USE

You can use present and future hypothetical constructions
- to indicate theoretical rather than actual possibilities:

Actual Possibility	Implied Meaning
(a) If we **get** some free time, we **can go** to the movies.	There is a strong possibility that we **may get** free time.
Theoretical Possibility	
(b) If we **got** some free time this weekend, we **could go** to the movies.	The possibility of free time is not great, but we are discussing it anyway.
(c) If I **had** free time, I **would go** to the movies.	There is no possibility of free time, but this is what would happen if there were.

• to be more polite:

Very Direct/Less Polite	Less Direct/More Polite
(d) The room **will** be much more comfortable if we **open** a window.	**(e)** The room **would** be much more comfortable if we **opened** a window.
(f) If you **have** time, **can** you help me with my homework tonight?	**(g)** If you **had** the time, **could** you help me with my homework tonight?
(h) I **won't** help you with your homework because I **have** to work tonight	**(i)** I **would** help you with your homework if I **didn't have to** work tonight.

You can discuss certain "sensitive" topics more easily and diplomatically by using hypothetical constructions. Using hypothetical indicates that you are not implying that the sensitive topic is actually true or could actually happen.

Nonhypothetical	Implied Meaning
(j) If someone **gives** you a lot of money, **will** you help them cheat on an important examination?	I think you might be the kind of person who will do something dishonest for money.
Hypothetical	
(k) If someone **gave** you a lot of money **would** you help them cheat on an important examination?	This is not a real situation, just an example. I don't think that you would do something dishonest for money.

The most common use of hypothetical statements in the Past Time Frame is to talk about things that did not actually happen.

Hypothetical	Implied Meaning
(l) Had you done your homework, you would have gotten an *A*.	You didn't get an *A* because you didn't do your homework.
(m) You could have brought a friend.	You had permission, but you came alone.
(n) You could have been more careful with your homework.	You had the ability, but you didn't do it.
(o) You should have seen the doctor.	You didn't do it.
(p) You might have cleaned the house before my mother got here.	It was still dirty when she arrived.
(q) I would have been here early, but the traffic was terrible!	I arrived late.

Exercise 17

Would you ever consider doing these things? Decide whether these statements represent actual or theoretical possibilities for you, and make a hypothetical or nonhypothetical sentence that reflects that.

> **EXAMPLE:** marry an American
>
> *If I marry an American, I will probably become a citizen.*
> *(actual possibility — something that might actually be possible for you)*
> *If I married an American, my parents would be very disappointed.*
> *(theoretical possibility — something that you don't think will ever be possible for you)*

1. go home for the next vacation
2. pass the TOEFL the next time you take it
3. become President of your country
4. have eight children
5. buy a new car within the next three months
6. join the army
7. get sick later today
8. look for a new place to live
9. have free time before class tomorrow

Exercise 18

Make these statements and requests more polite by using hypothetical conditionals.

> **EXAMPLE:** Don't smoke here.
>
> *I wouldn't smoke here if I were you.*

1. Can I close the door?
2. Do you mind turning down the radio a little bit?
3. Eat some more of this pie, because it will make the cook happy.
4. I won't come to your party.
5. I'm too busy to take the time to help you.

Exercise 19

Do these sentences indicate statements of past possibility or hypothetical events that did not happen?

> **EXAMPLES:** I didn't see him, but he could have been there.
> *past possibility*
> If John had been at the concert, he would have been able to explain how the composer was able to get those effects.
> *hypothetical event*

1. My brother could have loaned me the money, but he's too cheap.
2. Assuming that the plane was on time, it should have landed a little while ago.
3. I don't know what the problem is. They should have been here by now.
4. You should have asked for a receipt when you bought those clothes.
5. John might have worked a little harder on this report. It's pretty sloppy.
6. The thief might have gotten in through the window. It appears to be unlocked.

Focus 8

Other Common Verbs Used with Hypothetical Statements

MEANING
USE

- Use hypothetical constructions with **wish**. There is an important difference in meaning between the verbs **wish** and **hope**:
  - **Wish** describes situations that are not true:

	Implied Meaning
(a) I **wish** you **had come** to the lake last weekend.	You didn't come.
(b) I **wish** you **liked** Chinese food.	You don't like it.
(c) I **wish** you **would come** to my party.	You refuse to come.

- **Hope** expresses actual possibilities. The outcome can be in the past, present, or future:

	Implied Meaning
(d) I **hope** you **had** a nice time at the lake last weekend.	I don't know whether or not you did.
(e) I **hope** you **like** the new apartment.	I don't know if you will like it or not.
(f) I **hope** you'**ll come** to my party next week.	I don't know if you'll be able to come or not.

- You should use hypothetical constructions with verbs that indicate imagination or hypothetical supposition:
  - **(g)** **Let's imagine** that we **had** a new President.
  - **(h)** **Pretend** that you **could** fly. Do you think you **would** still own a car?
  - **(i)** **Suppose** we **went** to Europe next summer. How much do you think it **would** cost? (We are only talking about it now. We're not making an actual plan.)
- In formal English, you can use hypothetical constructions with **as if** (See Unit 12):
  - **(j)** John looks **as if** he **were** thinking about something else.
  - **(k)** He drank **as if** there **were** no tomorrow.
  - **(l)** You act **as if** there **were** no reason to be embarrassed.

Exercise 20

Refer to the Task. Write five sentences that identify the things Nadine Stair wishes she had done differently.

EXAMPLES: *Nadine Stair wishes that she had been more relaxed.*
She wishes she had dared to make more mistakes.

Activities

Activity 1

They say that everyone has 20/20 hindsight vision. Things that may have been unclear when they were happening seem very clear when we look back on the experience.

- Think about some things that you would have done differently if you had known then the things that you know now.
- Make a list of
    - things you wish you had done that you didn't do.
    - things you wish you hadn't done that you did do.
- Write an essay about your hindsight or make a presentation to the rest of the class.

Activity 2

If you could have three wishes, what would they be and why would you wish them?

- Write down your three wishes.
- Compare your answers to those of someone else in class. What do someone else's wishes tell you about his or her life? What do your wishes tell someone else about you?
- Make one statement about **why** you think your partner made the wishes that he or she did. Tell that statement to your partner but not to the rest of the class.

Activity 3

Suppose that you had just been made Supreme Commander of the Entire World. What actions would you take to

    end world hunger
    develop renewable energy sources
    control population growth
    protect the environment
    abolish war
    ensure political stability
    maintain economic growth

- Choose one of these areas and devise a plan for things you would do if you had the power and resources to accomplish them.
- Report your hypothetical plan to the rest of the class.

Activity 4

What would you do for ten million dollars? Would you tell a lie? Would you betray a friend? Would you give a child up for adoption? Would you become a citizen of another country? Would you leave your family? What would you refuse to do, even if you were offered ten million dollars?

- Identify some things you would and would not do for ten million dollars and compare them to those of other people in class.

Activity 5

A *dilemma* is a problem for which there are a limited number of possible solutions that are all unsatisfactory for one reason or another.

- What would you do if you were faced with the following dilemmas:

   Your parents do not approve of the person you want to marry.

   Your friend and you both work at the same company. You feel very loyal to the company, but you find out that your friend has stolen some of the company's money.

   You have fallen in love with the husband or wife of your best friend.

   Your best friend needs to borrow some money "for a serious emergency," but he or she will not say what that emergency is. You had been planning to spend that money to buy a birthday present for your boyfriend or girlfriend. Your friend needs the money right away, and the birthday celebration is also today. You cannot get any other money, only what you have now.

- Discuss your solutions with others in a small group.
- Devise a list of general strategies or suggestions about what people can do if they are faced with any kind of dilemma.
- Present your list of strategies to the rest of the class.

Sensory Verbs

Task

Seeing is the sense that we rely on most. But when we are deprived of sight, our other senses become sharper. Test your other senses through the following exercise:

- Go to a place you know well. It could be this classroom, a favorite room in your house, or someplace outdoors. Close your eyes and keep them closed for three minutes. Listen for the sounds that you can hear, both inside and outside. Are there any smells that you notice? Are they pleasant or unpleasant? What can you feel? Is it hot or cold? Can you feel a draft?
- Make a list of things you have noticed about this place that you never noticed when your eyes were open.

  I heard . . . .

  I smelled . . . .

  I felt . . . .

- Compare your list with several other people's lists. As a group, decide what other kinds of things escape your attention when you can rely on eyesight for information about the world around you.
- Present your ideas to the rest of the class.

Focus 1

Describing Two Actions

MEANING

- Sensory verbs (also known as verbs of observation) are similar to Pattern 2 verbs that take infinitive and gerund complements. You can use them to report the observed action of a "second subject." The second subject can be a noun or an object pronoun.

Sensory Verb	Second Subject	Observed Action
(a) I **saw**	the dog	jump into the water.
(b) Mary **heard**	us	laughing.

Exercise 1

Identify the sensory verbs in the following sentences. Restate the observed action as a separate sentence.

EXAMPLE: Mary saw the dog come into the room and steal the cheese.

sensory verb: saw; observed action: The dog came into the room and stole the cheese.

1. If you listen carefully, you can hear the birds singing in that tree.
2. Marlon likes to feel the wind blow through his hair when he rides his motorcycle.
3. Peter heard his voice get louder as he argued with Denise.
4. I saw the thief pick up the man's briefcase and begin to run away.
5. The doctor listened to the old woman complain about her arthritis.
6. When Deborah heard the baby crying, she hurried into the nursery.
7. We watched squirrels gathering nuts for the winter.
8. I smell something burning, so we had better check the stove.

Exercise 2

Answer these questions by using sensory verbs with a second subject.

EXAMPLE: What can you see at a disco?
You can see people dancing.

1. What can you hear at a concert?
2. What can you see at a skating rink?
3. What can you smell at a bakery?
4. What can you hear at the beach?
5. What can you see at a shopping mall?
6. What will you hear at a playground?
7. What can you hear in an English class?
8. What can you see at a gym?

Focus 2

FORM ● MEANING

Actions in Progress versus Completed Actions

FORM
MEANING

- Unlike *verb + gerund* or *verb + infinitive* combinations, sensory verbs use either a **present participle (verb + *ing*)** or the **simple form** of a verb to express the second action:

  (a) The teacher heard us **laughing**.

  (b) NOT: The teacher heard **our laughing**.

  (c) The teacher heard us **laugh**.

  (d) NOT: The teacher heard us **to laugh**.

- Depending on the form that is used, there is a difference in meaning and use. Using *-ing* **form** indicates that the action was **in progress or unfinished** at the time of observation. Using the **simple form** indicates that the **complete action** was observed in its entirety.

Action in Progress/Unfinished	Complete Action
(e) Bob heard the thieves **breaking** into the house, so he called the police.	**(f)** Bob **saw** the thieves **load** the TV into the car and **drive** away.

- In many cases, there is little difference in meaning, but in some cases the situation requires one form instead of the other.

Same Meaning	Different Meaning
(g) I watched the boys **playing** baseball in the park next door.	**(i)** I saw Mary **leaving** school, **so I ran to catch her.**
(h) I watched the boys **play** baseball in the park next door.	**(j)** I saw Mary **leave** school, so **I'm sure she's not coming to the teachers' meeting.**

Exercise 3

Decide on which form of the verb to use, based on the context, and underline it. In some sentences, both forms may be possible, so prepare to explain your choice.

EXAMPLE: I saw smoke (come/<u>coming</u>) from the storeroom, so I called the fire department.

1. I heard the phone (ring/ringing), but I decided not to answer it.
2. The principal watched the students (take/taking) the test so that she could be sure there was no cheating.
3. Matt felt himself (get/getting) angry as he and his roommate argued about who should do the dishes.
4. On my way to the store, I saw Morris (ride/riding) his new bike.
5. As Mary listened to the radio (play/playing) her favorite song, she began to cry and hurried out of the room.
6. I heard the workers (leave/leaving) earlier today. I'm sure they haven't returned yet.
7. We could all smell something (burn/burning). Apparently somebody had tossed a lighted cigarette into the wastepaper basket.

Exercise 4

Restate the numbered sentences in these paragraphs as sensory verb complements:

EXAMPLE: Here is what Tom saw: (1)Three boys were swimming in the river. (2)They were splashing and playing. (3)One of them shouted that it was time to go. (4)They picked up their towels and left.

(1)Tom saw three boys swimming in the river. (2)He watched them splashing and playing. (3)He heard one of them shout that it was time to go. (4)He watched them pick up their towels and leave.

1. Here is what Doris observed: (1)A man came into the bank. (2)He got in line. When he reached the teller's window, he handed her a piece of paper and a brown paper bag. (3)The teller was putting money in the bag, when a loud alarm began to ring. (4)Guards rushed in, but the man had escaped through the side entrance.
2. When Mrs. McMartin looked out the window, this is what she saw: (1)There were a few children playing on the swings. (2)Others were climbing on the monkeybars. (3)One little boy was running very fast around and around the playground. (4)Suddenly he fell down. (5)He screamed in pain. (6)All the other children looked around to see where the noise was coming from. (7)One child ran toward Mrs. McMartin's office.
3. Here is what I saw, heard, and felt during the hurricane. (1)The wind grew louder. (2)The windows and doors shook. (3)The trees swayed in the garden outside. I thought the house was moving. (4)A tree crashed against the house. (5)There was a sound of breaking glass upstairs. I went upstairs. (6)Rain was pouring through the broken window. (7)A strong wind blew into the room. (8)The wind howled louder and louder.

Focus 3

Present Participle versus Simple Form

MEANING

- You can use present participles (**verb** + **–ing**) instead of simple verbs
  - to indicate repeated action instead of a single occurrence:

Repeated Action	Single Action
(a) I saw the woman **slapping** her child.	**(b)** I saw the woman **slap** her child.
(c) The police watched the demonstrators **overturning trucks** and setting **them** on fire.	**(d)** The police watched the demonstrators **overturn a truck** and set **it** on fire.

  - with verbs of position, if the "second subject" is an inanimate object that cannot move by itself:
    - **(e)** I saw the bicycle **lying** by the side of the road.
    - **(f)** NOT: I saw the bicycle **lie** by the side of the road.
  - with verbs of interception (**find, catch, discover,** etc.), when the second action is interrupted or not completed:
    - **(g)** We **caught** the thief **taking** money out of the cash register.
    - **(h)** NOT: We caught the thief **take** money out of the cash register.
    - **(i)** We **found** the watchman **sleeping** at his desk.
    - **(j)** NOT: We found the watchman **sleep** at his desk.

Exercise 5

Choose the correct form of the verb given. In some cases, both answers may be correct, so prepare to explain why you chose your answer:

1. Brian heard the phone (ring/ringing), but by the time he reached it the person at the other end had hung up.
2. As the hurricane grew stronger, they heard many branches of the big oak tree (snap/snapping) and (fall/falling) to the ground.
3. John was relieved when he saw his lost wallet (sit/sitting) next to his checkbook on the shelf.
4. Mary watched the snow (fall/falling) gently through the trees.
5. Deborah heard Evan (cry/crying), so she went in to see what was wrong.
6. We heard the sound of laughter (drift/drifting) across the lake from the house where the party was.
7. When we arrived, we found the dog (wait/waiting) at the door for us.
8. I smell something (burn/burning). Did you remember to take the cookies out of the oven?

Activities

Activity 1

Describe this picture. Begin each sentence with "I see...."

Activity 2

In the Task, you had an opportunity to experience the world as a blind person does. How are blind people able to move around independently? In what ways do they compensate for lack of sight? How do they get information about where they are and where they are going? Consider people who cannot hear. How are they able to communicate with each other and the rest of the world?

- Discuss ways that people with sensory handicaps can compensate for those handicaps. Use your experience in the Task and any other experiences you have had with people who are blind or deaf.
- Present your ideas in a written or oral report.

Activity 3

Here are some general statements about human nature.

> People are generally in too much of a hurry.
> Children are spontaneous.
> Teenagers like to associate together in groups.
> Older people are generally slower than younger people.

Do you think such generalizations are true or not? This is an opportunity for you to test the validity of such generalizations through systematic observation.

- Choose a generalization that you want to test. It could be one of the statements listed above or some other generalization. You may want to test some generalization that involves cultural differences, such as "Americans are very outgoing" or "Asians are studious."
- Go to a place where you can watch lots of people. A shopping mall, a cafeteria, or a busy corner are all good places. Watch how people behave. Look for examples of behavior that reflect the generalization you are testing. Find as many examples as you can that either support or contradict the generalization and write a paragraph describing what you have observed.

    Here's an example:

    "They say that most people are generally friendly, and I have found that this seems to be true. At the mall yesterday, I saw many people smiling at each other. I saw two people meet by chance. They must have been old friends, because I saw them hug each other. I heard many people laughing and joking. I heard many of the salespeople say "Have a nice day" to customers. I saw one family arguing with each other, but strangers tended to be polite.

Activity 4

Have you ever been in a really strong storm, or a flood, or an earthquake, or some other large-scale natural disaster? Write a paragraph describing your experience and what you saw, heard, and felt.

24

Causative Verbs

Task

How do you think children should be raised? What things should good parents do to give their children a good upbringing? What is the best way to teach children responsibility? What is the best way to reward and punish? Answers to questions like these can vary from culture to culture.

- Think about the way your parents raised you. Did you ever hear your parents say:
  "We're doing this for your own good."
  "Everyone needs to do something for the family."
  "You can do this because we know you enjoy it."
- Thinking about these situations will help you identify strategies your parents used to try to give you a good upbringing. Consider these questions:

  What things did your parents make you do that you did not want to do?
  What things did they have you do on a regular basis that you did not mind doing but probably would not have done on your own?
  What things did they let you do as a reward for good behavior?
- Try to think of at least three answers for each question. For each thing you remember, decide whether or not it was an effective strategy, and whether you will use (or are using) this strategy as you raise you own children.
- Ask these questions of other students in the class to find out about their own experiences and opinions. Collect information from at least three other people. Here is a checklist to help you organize your information:

Discipline/ Punishment A	Responsibilities B	Rewards/ Motivations C	Effective? yes/no/why	Will You Use It? yes/no/why
Example: (1) no TV for a week (2) spanking (3) no allowance	(1) cut the grass (2) sweep the sidewalk (3) take care of younger sister	(1) allowance $5 per week (2) stay up late on weekends (3) ice cream and candy		
Student A: A1_____ A2_____ A3_____ _____ _____ _____ _____ _____ _____	_____ _____ _____ B1_____ B2_____ B3_____ _____ _____ _____	_____ _____ _____ _____ _____ _____ C1_____ C2_____ C3_____	_____ _____ _____ _____ _____ _____ _____ _____ _____	_____ _____ _____ _____ _____ _____ _____ _____ _____

Discipline/ Punishment A	Responsi- bilities B	Rewards/ Motivations C	Effective? yes/no/why	Will You Use It? yes/no/why
Student B:				
A1_____	_____	_____	_____	_____
A2_____	_____	_____	_____	_____
A3_____	_____	_____	_____	_____
_____	B1_____	_____	_____	_____
_____	B2_____	_____	_____	_____
_____	B3_____	_____	_____	_____
_____	_____	C1_____	_____	_____
_____	_____	C2_____	_____	_____
_____	_____	C3_____	_____	_____
Discipline/ Punishment A	Responsi- bilities B	Rewards/ Motivations C	Effective? yes/no/why	Will You Use It? yes/no/why
Student C:				
A1_____	_____	_____	_____	_____
A2_____	_____	_____	_____	_____
A3_____	_____	_____	_____	_____
_____	B1_____	_____	_____	_____
_____	B2_____	_____	_____	_____
_____	B3_____	_____	_____	_____
_____	_____	C1_____	_____	_____
_____	_____	C2_____	_____	_____
_____	_____	C3_____	_____	_____

- Based on your findings, make ten recommendations for parents.
  Start five of them with **"Parents should . . . ."**
  Start five recommendations with **"Parents shouldn't . . . ."**
- Compare your recommendations to those of the people you interviewed. Decide on a list of recommendations that you all agree on and present the list to the rest of the class.
- Compile a list of recommendations that the entire class agrees upon.

Focus 1

Causative Verbs and Pattern 2
Verbs with Causative Meaning

FORM
MEANING

- Sentences with causative verbs (*make, let, have, help*) are similar to sentences with pattern 2 verbs (verb + noun phrase + infinitive). You can use them in situations in which the subject of the main verb causes the object of the main verb, the second subject, to perform a second action. But causative verbs are slightly different: The **simple form of the verb**, rather than the infinitive, expresses the second action. This group is limited to a few verbs, but they are used very frequently.

Verb + Noun Phrase + Infinitive	Causative Verb
(a) Parents should **require** their children **to brush** their teeth before bedtime.	**(b)** Parents should **make** their children **brush** their teeth before bedtime.
(c) They shouldn't **allow** them **to misbehave in school.**	**(d)** They shouldn't **let** them **misbehave** in school.

- Causative meanings indicate how much **force** or **persuasion** is necessary to cause the person to do the action.
  - *Make*

	Implied meaning
(e) Parents should **make** naughty children **stand** in the corner instead of spanking them.	Parents should **force** naughty children to stand in the corner **against their will**.
Pattern 2 verbs with a similar meaning are *require, force, order, demand,* and *compel*.	

  - *Get*

	Implied Meaning
(f) Parents should **get** their children **to read** instead of watching TV.	Parents should **persuade rather than force** their children to read instead of watching TV.
This verb does not follow the usual pattern. It requires an infinitive rather than a simple verb. Other Pattern 2 verbs with a similar meaning are *persuade, convince, inspire, motivate,* and *encourage*.	

  - *Have*

	Implied Meaning
(g) Parents should **have** the doctor **examine their children at least once** a year.	Parents should **routinely employ or hire** a doctor to examine their children.
Pattern 2 verbs with a similar meaning are *hire, employ,* and *engage*.	

- *Let*

	Implied Meaning
(h) Good parents **let** their children **play** outside on sunny days.	Parents want their children to play outside and should **allow** them to do so.
Pattern 2 verbs with a similar meaning are *allow* and *permit*	

- *Help*

	Implied Meaning
(i) Good parents **help** their children **learn good manners.** **(j)** Good parents **help** their children **to learn good manners.**	Parents should **assist and participate with** their children in learning good manners.
You can use this verb with either simple verb complement or with an infinitive. A Pattern 2 verb with a similar meaning: *assist*	

Exercise 1

a) Underline the causative verbs and the verb + infinitive constructions with a causative meaning in this passage. Mark the various elements with the letters given: *(a)* the causer, *(b)* the causative verb, *(c)* the doer, and *(d)* the action. Is the action marked by an infinitive or a simple verb? One sentence has been done for you as an example.

(1)Kilroy hated his life in the army from the very first day. (2)When he arrived at Fort Dix for
                                  (a)   *(b) (c)*   *(d)*
basic training, <u>a drill instructor</u> <u>had</u> <u>him</u> <u>join all the other new recruits</u> on the parade ground.

(3)The officers made them stand in the hot sun for several hours, while clerks filled out forms.

(4)They would not allow the new recruits to joke or talk to each other, or even to move their

heads. (5)Then they had Army barbers cut their hair so short that Kilroy felt like he was bald.

(6)An officer ordered Kilroy to report to a long building called Barracks B, along with about

20 other men. (7)The sergeant at Barracks B had each man choose a bunk. (8)He let them put

their personal possessions in lockers next to each bunk. (9)Kilroy helped the man in the next

bunk make his bed, and that man helped Kilroy to do the same thing. (10)The sergeant then required the recruits to sweep the floors and clean the bathrooms. (11)Kilroy had wanted to join the army to learn how to be a soldier, but now he was beginning to worry that the army would only teach him how to be a janitor.

Exercise 2

Decide whether you think the policies suggested below are good ideas or not. Make statements with *should* or *shouldn't*, depending on whether you agree or disagree with the policy. Then supply a reason with *because* to explain why you feel the way you do. The first one has been done for you as an example.

> **EXAMPLE:** *Parents should let their kids play actively every day, because vigorous physical exercise is important for growing bodies.*

Causer	Causative Verb	Doer of Action	Action
EXAMPLE: parents	let	kids	play actively
1. parents	make	children	go to bed at 6:00
2. teachers	help	students	learn things by themselves
3. police	allow	people	break laws
4. ministers	get	rowdy teenagers	come to church
5. people	have	a dentist	examine their teeth regularly
6. dog owners	let	pets	run around freely
7. the law	require	everybody	pay taxes
8. a government	require	all citizens	take drug tests
9. a good manager	allow	employees	do whatever they like
10. a good manager	motivate	employees	do their best

Exercise 3

Match the verbs listed in Group A with the verbs in Group B that have the same or similar meaning.

GROUP A	GROUP B
let	convince
help	hire
have	require
get	employ
make	permit
	assist
	encourage

Exercise 4

What should a teacher do in order to help students learn to speak English? Make sentences stating your opinion, using each of the causative verbs given in Exercise 3. Be careful to use the correct form (infinitive or simple verb).

> **EXAMPLE:** *Teachers should* **have** *students do homework every night.*
> *Teachers should* **help** *students guess the meaning of unfamiliar vocabulary.*

Exercise 5

What are the basic responsibilities of a government and the people it governs? For each statement of causer/doer/action listed, choose an appropriate causative that expresses your opinion. Write two complete sentences expressing that opinion: one with a causative verb and one with verb+infinitive complement.

> **EXAMPLE: causer:** government **doer:** citizens **action:** vote in regular elections
> *Governments should let their citizens vote in regular elections.*
> *Governments should allow their citizens to vote in regular elections.*

Causer	Doer	Action
government	citizens	• pay taxes • read any books and magazines they wish • be of service to the nation • meet national goals • defend the country
citizens	government	• be responsive to their wishes • work without corruption • establish national goals • maintain law and order • provide for basic defense

Focus 2

Passive Causative Verbs

FORM

- The causatives *make* and *help* and all Pattern 2 verbs with causative meaning can be made passive.

Active Causative Verbs	Passive Causative Verbs
(a) Parents should **make** their children **brush** their teeth before bedtime.	(b) Children should **be made to brush** their teeth before bedtime.
(c) Parents should **allow** children to have their own bank accounts.	(d) Children should **be allowed** to have their own bank accounts.
(e) Parents should **require** children to go to bed at a certain time.	(f) Children should **be required** to go to bed at a certain time.
(g) Parents should **help** their children **learn** good table manners.	(h) Children should **be helped to learn** good table manners.

- The passive is especially common when the causer of the action is understood or not stated, or is a law or an institution:
    - (i) All children are required to go to school.
    - (j) Minors aren't allowed to drink alcoholic beverages.
- When the verbs *make* and *help* are passive, their complements must be stated as infinitives, not simple verbs.
    - (k) Students should **be made to study**.
    - (l) NOT: Students should be **made study**.
    - (m) Children should **be helped to understand** good manners.
    - (n) NOT: Children should be **helped understand** good manners.
- The other common causatives, *get, have,* and *let* do not appear as passive verbs in causative sentences.
    NOT: Children should **be gotten** to read.
    NOT: Teachers should **be had** to teach.
    NOT: Children shouldn't **be let** to stay up too late.

Exercise 6

Decide whether the causative verbs in these sentences can be made passive without losing information or being ungrammatical. If so, write the passive version of the sentence.

EXAMPLES: The law requires parents to send their children to school.
Parents are required to send their children to school.

The doctor got the patient to take the bitter tasting medicine.
No change possible.

1. Tradition doesn't allow people to smoke in church.
2. Lack of time forced Kilroy to return to the barracks before the movie was over.
3. The law requires everyone who works to pay some income taxes.
4. People shouldn't let their dogs run free around the neighborhood
5. We had the janitor clean up the mess.
6. When I was a child, my mother didn't allow me to play in the street.

Focus 3

Passive Action Verbs

FORM
USE

- You can also use the passive voice with verbs that express the second action when the agent is understood or not important. There are some differences in form depending on which causative you use.
- For Pattern 2 verbs with causative meaning use a passive infinitive.

Active Action Verb	Passive Action Verb
(a) Parents should **require** their **children to finish homework** before TV time.	**(b)** Parents should require **homework to be finished** before TV time.
(c) Parents should **encourage** children **to do homework** carefully.	**(d)** Parents should encourage **homework to be done** carefully.

- With the causative *let*, omit *to* from the infinitive.

(e) Parents shouldn't **let** their children **be** neglected.	**(f)** NOT: Parents shouldn't **let** their children **to be** neglected.

- With the causative verbs *have* or *get*, you only need the past participle.

Active Action Verb	Passive Action Verb
(g) I had the barber cut my hair.	**(h)** I had my hair **cut**. **(i)** NOT: I had my hair **to be cut**.
(j) I got the judge to reduce my fine.	**(k)** I got my fine **reduced**. **(l)** NOT: I got my fine **to be reduced**.

- You can also use **had** and **get** to indicate simple passive meaning. (See Unit 4) Therefore, in some cases the meaning can be ambiguous:

Causative Meaning (Subject is the Agent)	Simple Passive Meaning (Subject is the Recipient)
(m) Mary had her car washed. **(o)** Mary got the thief arrested.	**(n)** Mary had her car stolen. (Someone stole Mary's car.) **(p)** Mary got herself arrested. (Mary was arrested)

Exercise 7

(a) Restate all the passive causatives in this paragraph as active constructions. Use *officers* as a probable agent. Sentence 1 has been done for you as an example.

Example: *Once again officers required the recruits to stand in the hot sun...*

(b) Sentence 4 is an example of passive meaning, not causative meaning. Can you restate this sentence so that the causative meaning is not ambiguous?

Kilroy's second day in the army was not much better than his first. (1) Once again the recruits were required to stand in the hot sun for several hours while clerks filled out even more forms. (2) They still weren't allowed to talk to each other, and they weren't allowed to sit down. (3) Next they were ordered to go to the medical building. (4) There they had their teeth examined and got their blood pressure measured. (5) Next was a test of physical endurance, where they were forced to run three miles in the hot sun. (6) Recruits who didn't run fast enough were required to run an extra mile as punishment. (7) By the time Kilroy was allowed to return to his bunk at the barracks, he was so tired he could barely walk. (8) As he lay on his bunk, he was sorry that he had been persuaded to join the army. (9) That night the men were allowed to write letters to their families, but Kilroy was too tired to do anything but sleep.

Exercise 8

Are these sentences correct or incorrect? For incorrect sentences, identify the mistake and fix it.

1. The students were got to do their homework.
2. The sergeant made the recruits to march for several hours.
3. A tailor was had to shorten my trousers.
4. Parents shouldn't let their children to watch too much television.
5. I had the waiter to bring the food to the table.
6. They encouraged all their children be independent.
7. Parents should make their children to brush their teeth.
8. Companies should be required to provide their employees with health insurance.
9. The babysitter made the children to fall a sleep by singing quietly.
10. Kilroy had his hair to be cut.

Activities

Activity 1

What routine jobs do you hate? Pretend that you do not have to worry about money. What things would you have other people do for you?

- Decide on 5 to 10 personal tasks that you would have someone else do, if money were no object. (For example: If money were no object, I would have somebody else do my grammar homework.)
- Compare your list to those of other students in class. What chores does everyone hate doing?
- Based on the other lists you have seen, what are the three most unpopular chores that people have to do on a regular basis?

Activity 2

In the Task, you examined the way people raise children. You identified things that parents should and should not do. Based on your discussion and your own experiences, state your opinion on this question:

Do good parents **make** their children do things or **get** their children to do things?

- Write a brief essay that explains your opinion, and why you feel the way you do. Support your opinion with examples from your own or other people's lives.

Activity 3

Based on the interviews that you conducted in the Task, did you find any interesting cultural or family patterns in the child-rearing practices of your classmates?

- Write a brief essay explaining any differences you found between the way children are raised in your own culture or family and some of the other culture or family patterns you learned about in the process of doing the Task.

Activity 4

There is a saying in English, "You can catch more flies with honey than you can with vinegar." What do you think are the best ways to get someone to do something? Support your ideas by describing a situation in which someone convinced you to do something you did not initially want to do. How did that person convince you? Were you glad you did it, or not?

Activity 5

If you were the leader of the country, what things would you change?

What laws would you establish for people to follow?
What would you require people to do?
What privileges would you allow people?
What things would you not allow them to do?
How would you get people to support you?

- Think of at least three answers to each of these questions, and present the information to the rest of the class in an oral presentation, explaining why they should let you be their leader.
- Take a vote to see who was the most convincing candidate.

25

Articles in Discourse

Task

Proverbs are well-known sayings that express general truths. They come into existence because many people in similar situations have seen similar results. Proverbs represent general lessons that many people have learned from actual individual experiences.

- Here are a number of proverbs. Choose one that you agree with, and think of an example from your own life (or that of someone that you know) that proves the truth of the proverb. Write a paragraph about that experience. The first proverb has been done for you as an example. Tell your own story to illustrate that proverb or another from the list.

A dog is man's best friend.	The leopard cannot change his spots.
Time is money.	Actions speak louder than words.
A fool and his money are soon parted.	Beauty is only skin-deep.
Experience is the best teacher.	Every cloud has a silver lining.
An idle mind is the devil's playground.	Time heals all wounds.
	Money is the root of all evil.
Absence makes the heart grow fonder.	A man is known by the company he keeps.

A dog is man's best friend. I once had a dog named Poppy. She was a very faithful friend. Every afternoon when I came home, the dog would greet me with kisses and a wagging tail. I liked the wagging tail, but I didn't enjoy the kisses very much. Even so, she was always glad to see me, and I was happy to see her too. There was a time in my life when I was feeling very lonely. I didn't think I had any friends. Every day I came home to an empty house with an empty heart. But Poppy was always at the door waiting for me. She seemed to know whenever I was sad or lonely, and at those times she would be extra friendly. One time she even gave me a gift: an old bone. Somehow she knew that I was especially sad. She must have thought the bone would cheer me up. Those bad times passed eventually, but they would have been a lot more difficult without my faithful companion, Poppy. She proved to me that a dog really is a wonderful friend.

Focus 1

Determiners in English

FORM

- Most noun phrases in English require a determiner. Determiners can be
  - **demonstratives:**
    (a) We need **this** pen. **That** pen is out of ink.
  - **possessives:**
    (b) **Peter's** information surprised us more than **his** appearance.
  - **quantifiers:**
    (c) Denise has **few** friends. She doesn't make **much** effort.
  - **articles:**
    (d) Denise has **a** new position. She has **some** work to do. She feels **the** work is quite important.
- There is only one determiner in each noun phrase.
  (e) NOT: Here is **a this** pen.
  (f) NOT: **That my** pen is green.

Exercise 1

Underline and identify the determiners in the sample paragraph of the Task. Are they demonstratives, possessives, quantifiers, or articles? Are the nouns count or non-count, singular or plural?

Focus 2

FORM

Definite and Indefinite Articles

FORM

- There are three indefinite articles:
  - *a/an:* used with singular-count nouns: *a* precedes nouns (or their modifiers) that begin with a consonant sound; *an* precedes nouns (or their modifiers) that begin with a vowel sound.

a book	a shiny apple	an uncomfortable
a church	an apple	situation
a hotel	an honest man	an hour
a university	an easy lesson	

327

- *some:* used with plural count nouns and non-count nouns to indicate a quantity or amount:
  - **(a)** I need some pencils.
  - **(b)** Some teachers will be arriving soon.
  - **(c)** I have some ideas about the party.
  - **(d)** Would you like some rice?
  - **(e)** Some water got on my notebook.
  - **(f)** I'm looking for some information.
- **No article (∅):** used with plural count nouns and non-count nouns in generic statements that do **not** refer to a quantity or amount. (See Focus 6 for other rules regarding **some** vs. ∅)
  - **(g)** Everyone needs **friends.**
  - **(h)** Teachers want **students** to succeed.
  - **(i)** **Ideas** can come from anywhere.
  - **(j)** **Rice** is eaten all over Asia.
  - **(k)** **Water** is necessary for life.
  - **(l)** I'm looking for **information** about public transportation.
- There is one definite article: **the.** You can use it with all nouns, count and non-count, singular and plural.

Focus 3

Generic versus Particular Statements

- Using articles depends on whether we are making a **generic** statement or a **particular** statement. In order to know which article you can use, you must first decide whether a sentence is particular or generic.
  - **Generic statements** talk about **concepts and ideas** and refer to **general classes or categories.** Such statements are true for the class or category and therefore they are also true for all members of that class.
  - **Particular statements** talk about **real situations** and refer to **actual members or items of a class or category.** Such statements are true only for the member, not necessarily the category itself.

- Compare these pairs of sentences:

Generic Statements	Particular Statements
(a) The lion is found throughout Africa. (a category of animal)	**(b)** I saw **the lion** at the circus. (a particular animal—not all lions are in the circus.)
(c) Bicycles are an excellent means of transportation. (a category)	**(d)** They went shopping for **bicycles** yesterday. (particular things they wanted to buy—they didn't buy all the bicycles in the world.)
(e) An angry customer is a frightening sight. (a category of person)	**(f)** We saw **an angry customer** complaining about the high price of tickets. (a particular person—not all customers are angry.)
(g) Some people never fall in love. (a category of people)	**(h) Some people** are joining us for dinner. (particular people, not a class of people)
(i) Information is increasingly communicated by electronic rather than printed media. (a category of things that things that are communicated electronically)	**(j)** Please give me **some information** on medical treatments for heart disease. (particular written or spoken facts)

- The rules for article use depend on whether the noun phrase occurs in a generic statement or a particular statement.
  - In generic statements, you can use both definite and indefinite articles in many of the same kinds of sentences.

    (k) The lion is a mighty creature.
    (l) A lion is a mighty creature.
    (m) ∅ **Lions** are mighty creatures.
    (n) Any large zoo will surely have **some lions** as part of its collection.
  - In particular statements, the use of articles depends on whether a noun is specific or nonspecific.

Exercise 2

Decide whether the highlighted noun phrases in these sentences are generic (refer to classes or categories) or particular (members of a class).

> **EXAMPLE:** An idle mind is **the devil's playground.**
>
> *generic*
>
> There is **a playground** next to the school down the street.
>
> *particular*

1. I wish we had **some mangoes** for the fruit salad, but they're so expensive!
2. **Mangoes** are a fruit found in most tropical places.
3. I saw **a doctor** about my cough.
4. **A doctor** is someone who has received training in medical science.
5. **Computers** have completely changed the way we live.
6. Don't go to that store for **computers.** They're cheaper at Smith Electronics.
7. **Many people** don't like spicy food.
8. There weren't **many people** at Jane's party.
9. If you really want to know how John is feeling, don't ask **the doctor**, ask **the nurses.** They will have better information.
10. Jane cooked a big pot of chili, but **many people** didn't eat it.
11. **Computers** are cheaper now than they were ten years ago.
12. There is a shortage of **nurses** in American hospitals today.
13. **Computers** for the new lab are being donated by **a company** in San Jose.
14. There aren't **many people** who actually like paying taxes.
15. Millions of people in this country can't afford to go to **the doctor** when they are sick.
16. **A company** needs to make sure that it is earning a profit.

Exercise 3

Write one generic sentence and one particular sentence for each of the cues listed here.

1. bicycles
2. a new car
3. the English language
4. transportation
5. tea
6. salespeople
7. books
8. hard work
9. Chinese food
10. trouble

Focus 4

Specific versus Nonspecific Nouns

MEANING

- In particular statements, article use is determined by whether a noun is specific or nonspecific.
  - Specific nouns require definite articles. Specific nouns refer to an identified object. Both the speaker and the listener know specifically which object is being referred to. Both writer and reader can form a mental image of that particular object.

Definite Article	Implied Meaning
(a) Please give me **the** red pen.	There is only one red pen.
(b) Please pass **the** tea.	There is a teapot right here.

- Nonspecific nouns require indefinite articles. A noun is nonspecific when either the speaker or the listener does not know specifically which object is being referred to.

Indefinite Article	Implied Meaning
(c) Please give me **a** red pen.	There are several pens. More than one of them are red. Any red pen is OK.
(d) Let's go to **a** restaurant and have **some** tea.	We don't know which restaurant it will be, or what kind of tea we will have.

- Use indefinite articles when
  - the speaker has a specific mental image of the noun, but the listener does not:

Indefinite Articles	Implied Meaning
(e) a/an: I bought **a new car.**	You haven't seen it yet.
(f) some: I had **some rice** for dinner last night.	I can remember it, but since you weren't there, you can't.
(g) Ø: There are **students** in my class who always do their homework.	I know which ones they are, but you don't.

  - the speaker does not have a specific mental image, but the listener does:

	Implied Meaning
(h) I hear you bought **a new car.** What kind is it?	You know, but I don't.
(i) You have **some mail** for me, don't you?	I don't know whether you do or not.
(j) Mary tells you **secrets** that she never tells me.	You know which secrets, but I don't.

331

• neither the speaker nor the listener has a specific mental image:

	Implied Meaning
(k) I hope we have **a wonderful time** on our vacation.	We don't know exactly what's going to happen.
(l) Let's get **some spaghetti** when we go out tonight.	We haven't decided on a restaurant.
(m) We should bring **food** to the picnic.	We haven't decided what kind.

Exercise 4

In the highlighted noun phrases, why was the particular article used? Indicate whether the noun was *(a)* specific for both speaker and listener, *(b)* specific for speaker but not listener, *(c)* specific for listener but not speaker, *(d)* nonspecific for both speaker and listener.

   EXAMPLE: Do you want to go to **a movie** tonight? *(d)*

1. The Simpsons just bought **a beautiful new house.** You really ought to see it. I'm sure you'll think it's wonderful.
2. I want you to meet **a friend** of mine. You both have the same interests.
3. Did you have **a good time** at **the party?**
4. Let's have **some friends** over for dinner on Saturday.
5. I heard Charley has **a new girlfriend.** What's she like?

Exercise 5

Choose the correct implication for each of these sentences. (*I* refers to the speaker or writer. *You* refers to the listener or reader.)

1. The student from Japan is here to see you.
    a) There are several students from Japan who had appointments.
    b) There is only one student from Japan who had an appointment.
2. Let's go to a restaurant.
    a) We have already decided which restaurant to go to.
    b) Let's choose a restaurant.
3. Did a teacher say anything about a test?
    a) I am asking about one class.
    b) I am asking about all my classes.
4. Some friends are coming to dinner.
    a) You know who is coming to dinner.
    b) You don't know who is coming to dinner.

5. Let's invite the neighbors to dinner.
   a) You know which neighbors will be invited to dinner.
   b) You don't know which neighbors will be invited to dinner.
6. You should see a doctor about that cough.
   a) I have a specific doctor in mind.
   b) Any doctor should be able to help you.

Exercise 6

Decide whether these sentences require definite or indefinite articles. Add the appropriate article *(a/an, the, some,* or *Ø)* in the blank spaces. There may be more than one correct answer. Prepare to state your reason for choosing a particular article.

1. I didn't bring _____ roses that you asked for. I completely forgot them.

2. Sally wanted to buy _____ new dress, so she's gone out to find one.

3. _____ teacher was here to see you. I think it was your English teacher.

4. Did you give _____ musicians a nice tip? They certainly played beautiful music

   for your party.

5. Would you like _____ cold ice tea?

6. How did you enjoy _____ Chinese food last night?

7. I have _____ problems that I don't want to talk about.

8. John sent Mary _____ card for her birthday, but she says she never received it.

9. _____ bank where Doris works was robbed by _____ masked man with

   _____ gun.

10. When _____ police arrived, it was too late. _____ robber had disap-

    peared.

Focus 5

Using Articles in Discourse

USE

- Most nouns are marked with an indefinite article the first time they are mentioned because they are nonspecific: It is the first time the listener or reader has encountered the reference. In subsequent sentences, that same noun is specific: Both speaker/writer and listener/reader now know exactly which noun is being refered to, so you should use a definite article.

    (a) There once was **a** little old man who lived in **a** shack by **a** river.
    The shack was rather shabby, and so was **the** man.

    (b) I once had **a** big black dog and **a** little white dog. **The** black dog kept itself very clean, but **the** white dog loved to roll in mud.

- Nouns become specific

    - by direct reference. The noun is repeated:

        (c) I had **a dog** named Poppy. Every afternoon when I came home, **the dog** would greet me with **kisses** and **a wagging tail**. I liked **the wagging tail**, but I didn't enjoy **the kisses** very much.

    - by indirect reference. The noun itself is not repeated, but the reference is still clear from the context:

        (d) If you have **a dog** as **a pet**, you can always look forward to going home because of **the kisses** and **the wagging tail** that are there to greet you when you arrive.

        (e) I read **an interesting book. The author** suggests that all life came from visitors from another planet. **The first chapter** recounts stories of visitors from outer space that are found in many different cultures.

Exercise 7

Write articles (a, an, Ø, some, the) in the blank spaces. More than one answer may be correct, so prepare to explain why you chose the answer you did.

1. I have _____ foolish friend who is really careless with _____ money.

He has _____ good-paying job, but he doesn't even have _____ bank account. He says he doesn't need one because he spends his salary right away. He gets

_____ paycheck once _____ week. _____ money is always gone before _____ week is over. I can't tell you what he spends it on. And you know

what? Neither can he!

2. I saw _____ "interesting" play last night. _____ actors were excellent, and _____ set was beautiful. However, _____ play itself was unfortunately not very well written.

3. Would you like _____ cake? _____ icing is _____ special recipe from _____ friend of my mother's. I made _____ cake and _____ icing myself.

4. Little Billy doesn't like _____ school. He says _____ teachers are boring. He doesn't like doing _____ homework. He much prefers to watch _____ cartoons on TV. As _____ result, his teachers aren't very happy with _____ way he performs in class. If he doesn't take _____ responsibility for doing _____ assignments, he may have to repeat _____ same grade next year.

Focus 6

USE

Repeating the Indefinite Article

USE

- There are certain situations in which you do not follow the usual rule of replacing an indefinite article with a definite article after the first time it is mentioned:
  - sentences with **there is/there are**.
    - **(a)** There once was **a** little old man who lived in **a** shack by *a river*. **The** shack was rather shabby, and so was **the** man. Although *there was a river* right next to **the** shack, **the** old man had to walk quite far to get clean drinking water.
  - sentences that identify someone or something as a member of a class or category:

	Implied Meaning
(b) I once had **a** dog. Her name was Poppy. She was **a** good dog.	She was a member of the category "good dogs."
(c) You know John. He's **a** teacher.	He's a member of the category "teachers."

- Do not use **some** for plural nouns that identify things as part of a group.

| (d) John is **a** teacher.
 John and Fred are teachers.
 (f) Paris is **a** city in Europe.
 Paris, Rome, and Munich are cities in Europe. | (e) NOT: John and Fred are **some** teachers.
 (g) NOT: Paris, Rome, and Munich are **some** cities in Europe. |

Exercise 8

Add the correct articles to the blank spaces in these sentences.

(1)I once had _____ experience that proved to me that _____ idle mind is _____ Devil's playground. Miss Kersell was my eighth grade science and math teacher. (2)She was _____ very strict teacher, and wouldn't allow any misbehaving in class. (3)To my friend Billy, this presented _____ tantalizing challenge. He found math and science very easy, so he was frequently bored in class. (4)As _____ result, he would try to play _____ tricks on her without getting caught. (5)It was _____ challenge that he could never resist, especially when he didn't have anything else to do. (6)One day we were taking _____ arithmetic quiz. (7)It was _____ easy quiz, but I have never been good at arithmetic, so it was taking me _____ long time. (8)But Billy had finished _____ quiz in just _____ few minutes. (9)I heard _____ strange noise coming from the back of the room. (10)It was _____ noise like no other I had ever heard. (11)Someone in _____ front of the class began to giggle. (12)Then there were _____ giggles in the back. (13)Soon there was _____ laughter everywhere. (14)Miss Kersell was furious, and looked everywhere to find out where _____ noise was coming from. (15)Billy had found _____ way to make _____ strange noise by rubbing his foot against _____ leg of his chair.

Focus 7

Unique Nouns

USE

- **Unique nouns** are specific for both the speaker and the listener without prior mention. This means that the **first** time they are mentioned, they are marked with a definite determiner. You do not need to introduce them in a nonspecific context.

    (a) I hear someone knocking at **the** door.

- A noun can be unique
    - because of a particular situation or setting:

Unique Nouns	Implied Meaning
(b) We were all having dinner. We were sitting around **the table**, and I asked my brother to pass **the butter**.	There was only one table and one dish of butter.
(c) "How did you do on **the exam** yesterday?" "Terrible! **The questions** were really difficult!"	There are two students in the same class. They both know which test is being referred to.
(d) This is going to be a wonderful vacation. I hope you remembered to ask **the neighbors** to pick up **the mail**.	We always ask the same neighbors each time we go away, and the mail is routinely delivered every day.

- because it is a universal reference:
    - **(e)** **The sky** is so beautiful tonight. **The moon** is bright, and **the stars** look like diamonds. (There is only one sky and one moon.)
    - **(f)** My dog used to love to roll in **the mud**.
    - **(g)** Let's go to **the beach. The ocean air** is supposed to be good for you.
- because of immediate identification by a relative clause or prepositional phrase:
    - **(h)** **The street where John lives** is lined with trees.
    - **(i)** First we went to a hotel where **the man at the desk** told us we had no reservations.
    - **(j)** **The book the teacher told us about** is available at **the bookstore across the street**.
- because it is identified by rank in a sequence:
    - **(k)** **The first time I ever went bowling**, I got **the highest score of anybody in the group**.

Exercise 9

Why do you think the highlighted nouns in the following sentences are unique? Decide if they are unique because of

    (a) prior reference (identify the reference);
    (b) a specific context or situation (identify the context or situation);
    (c) a universal context or situation;
    (d) being identified by a modifier (identify the modifier).

1. An idle mind is **the devil's** playground.
2. I saw a great movie last night. **The camera work** was fantastic.
3. **The newspaper** said it was going to rain tonight.
4. **The tallest mountain** in **the world** is on **the border** between Nepal and China.
5. **The place** we went last year is great for a vacation.
6. Let's go to **the club** for dinner tonight.
7. **The teacher** said we have to finish **the assignment** before Friday.
8. **The town** where I grew up was quite small.
9. **The noise** Billy made was like no other noise I had ever heard before.
10. What did **the doctor** say about **the medicine** you've been taking?

Exercise 10

Write the appropriate article *(a, an, the,* or Ø*)* in the blanks. There may be more than one correct choice, so prepare to explain why you have chosen the particular article.

(1)Peter Principle believes that every cloud has _____ silver lining. (2)He is

_____ very optimistic person. (3)He thinks that _____ problem is really

_____ opportunity in disguise. (4)As _____ result, he is always happy and

reasonably content with _____ things that _____ life has given him. (5)

_____ people like being around him, because he's _____ cheerful, positive

person.

    (6)Denise Driven is just _____ opposite. (7)She always looks on _____

dark side of _____ things. (8)If she encounters _____ problem, she some-

times blames it on _____ fact that she is _____ woman in _____

man's world. (9)She believes that _____ world isn't _____ fair place, and she, in particular, has always had _____ bad luck. (10)Although she's not _____ optimistic person, she doesn't spend much time feeling sorry for herself. (11)She rarely has time to listen to anyone's troubles or tell you about _____ troubles she is facing. (12)But whenever _____ friend does something nice for her, she always suspects that the person actually has _____ hidden motive. (13)She believes that every silver lining has _____ cloud.

Exercise 11

Write the appropriate article in the blanks. There may be more than one correct choice, so prepare to explain why you have chosen the particular article.

(1)The tall person in this picture is one of _____ most beautiful people I know, _____ woman by _____ name of Big Sue. (2)She proves _____ truth of _____ saying, "Beauty is only skin deep." (3)Perhaps people who don't know her well would say that she is not _____ beautiful person. (4)I guess that compared to _____ movie star or _____ fashion model, she isn't that attractive. (5)But anyone who knows her well thinks that she has _____ beautiful and courageous spirit. (6)Her beauty is in her personality. (7)She has _____ deep, booming laugh that makes other people laugh with her. (8)She's not self-conscious about her size.

(9)She makes _____ jokes about it. (10)She was _____ person who invented _____ name "Big Sue." (11)She says there are plenty of Sues in _____ world, but only one Big Sue. (12)If she gains _____ few pounds, she doesn't worry. (13)She just says, "There's more of me to love." (14)She is _____ incredible dancer, and moves around _____ dance floor with _____ grace and style. (15)She is _____ wonderful comedian. (16)She can tell _____ stories in _____ way that has _____ people falling down with laughter. (17)She has _____ friends all over _____ world. (18)She has turned down _____ dozens of proposals for marriage. (19)People can't help falling in love with her, once they get to know her well. (20)But she's not in _____ hurry to find _____ husband. She says, "I'll wait till I'm old and skinny. Right now I'm having too much fun."

Exercise 12

Write the appropriate article in the blanks. There may be more than one correct choice, so prepare to explain why you have chosen a particular article.

(1)When I first went to _____ university, I learned the truth of the proverb, "Absence makes _____ heart grow fonder." (2)It was _____ first time I had lived away from home. (3)I was surprised to discover how homesick I got, even after just _____ few days. (4)When I lived with my family, my brother and I used to fight about everything. (5)He wanted to watch one TV program and I wanted to watch another. (6)We fought about whose turn it was to do certain chores, like feeding _____ dog, sweeping _____ garage, cutting _____ grass, and taking out _____ garbage. (7)We argued about whose turn it was to use _____ car on Saturday night. (8)(I was allowed to use it one week, and then he was allowed to use it _____ other.) (9)But when I moved away, I realized that there were _____ lot of things about my brother that I missed. (10)I began to forget about all _____ tricks he used to play on me. (11)I started to remember only _____ happy times we had spent together. (12)By _____ time _____ year ended and I went back to spend _____ summer at home, I was really anxious to see him again.

Activities

Activity 1

Every country has different proverbs. In America, we say "Don't bite off more than you can chew," to remind people not to be too ambitious or try to do too many things at once. In Afghanistan, the same idea is expressed by the proverb, "You can't hold two watermelons in one hand."

- Work with a partner from a different cultural background and come up with three pairs of proverbs. Each pair should express the same idea in two different ways.
- Share the messages and the proverbs with the rest of the class.

Activity 2

Describe an object that you found once, and what you did with it. Compare your story with those of other people in the class. Can you devise a proverb that talks about finding objects and what should be done with them?

Activity 3

A time capsule is an airtight box (usually about one cubic meter) that is sometimes built into the foundation of a building. The designers of the time capsule fill it with objects that they think are important, interesting, or characteristic of the time when the building was built.

- Imagine that you are organizing a time capsule to be placed in a skyscraper being built today. The building is expected to remain standing for several hundred years. What objects would you place in the time capsule and why would you choose those particular objects?
- Work with several other people and decide on the contents of a time capsule that will not be opened for at least 500 years. Present your list of items and your reasons for choosing them to the rest of the class.

Activity 4

Write about three discoveries or inventions that have changed the course of history.

Activity 5

What are three things (objects) that everybody needs? Write a short composition describing your three choices and why you think everyone should have them. Start your essay with: **"There are three things everyone needs: . . . ."**

Activity 6

Here are four pictures. What story do you think they tell?

Demonstratives in Discourse

26

Task

Peter Principle and Denise Driven are having an argument. Peter wants to take the afternoon off to watch his youngest son perform in a Christmas pageant at school. Denise feels that he has already taken off too much time from work, and that she needs help in the office.

DD: Mr. Green has informed me that you're not going to be here this afternoon. **That's** outrageous, Peter! What about the Davis contract? **It's** due first thing Monday morning.

PP: Well, my son's in a Christmas play at school. **It's** his first big role. He's one of the Three Wise Men.

DD: He certainly didn't learn **that** role from his father! Is some stupid Christmas play more important than meeting the contract deadline?

PP: You'd better believe **it!** Besides, I spoke with Mr. Green. I told him **it** would get done sooner or later.

DD: If he believes **that**, he'll believe anything. **That's** what makes me so annoyed, Peter. **This** isn't the first time you've bailed out when there was a deadline. You're always asking for permission to take time off, and I get left holding the bag. I'm getting real tired of **it**, Peter. **It's** all I can do to keep this office running professionally!

PP: I'm sure Mr. Green would be happy to give you time off too. Just ask for **it**, Denise. **That's** all you have to do.

DD: **That's** not the point. **It's** true that most of us would probably rather be playing instead of working. But some of us have a sense of responsibility and a respect for hard work.

PP: **That's** true. My responsibility is to my son, and I respect the hard work he's put into learning his lines. **It's** not easy when you're only six years old.

DD: Don't give me **that** nonsense, Peter. I don't much fancy **it.**

PP: **That's** your trouble, Denise. You need a little nonsense in your life.

DD: My personal life is none of your business!

PP: Denise Driven has a personal life? Fancy **that!**

DD: **That's it!** I'm leaving. I'm lodging a formal complaint about **this** with Mr. Green.

PP: Well, **that's that**, then, isn't **it**? I guess there's nothing I can do to calm you down. I may as well leave a little early for the play. **It's** important to get there early, if you want to get a good seat.

- With a partner or in a small group, examine the use of *it, this*, and *that* in the previous dialogue. Important examples are highlighted for you. What is being referred to each time one of these forms is used? Can you substitute other forms? Does this change the meaning?
- What can you say about when native speakers use *it* instead of *that*? Decide on two things you have noticed and report them to the rest of the class.

Focus 1

FORM ● MEANING

Form and Meaning of Demonstratives

FORM
MEANING

- You can use demonstratives as determiners or as pronouns.
  (a) Does **this pencil** belong to you?
  (b) Yes, **that's** mine.
- The form of the demonstrative depends on whether the object is singular or plural and near or far.

	Near	Far
singular	**(a)** You should read **this book**. **(c) This** is delicious.	**(b)** Does **that pencil** belong to you? **(d)** Is **that** yours?
plural	**(e) These problems** aren't so serious. **(g)** If you like peaches, try **these**.	**(f) Those people** live down the street from my parents. **(h) Those** are the cutest puppies I have ever seen!

- Near and far distinctions are determined by
  - physical distance:
    (i) Please sit in **this** chair (**by me**). **That** chair (**over there**) is broken.
  - chronological distance:
    (l) I've been to two parties in the last week, but **this** one (today) is much more enjoyable than **that** party Denise had (a few days ago) at the Gun Club.
  - whether the speaker is involved with the situation or feels distanced from it:
    (m) What are we going to do about **this** budget deficit?
    (n) I don't know. **That's** for you to worry about, not me!

Focus 2

Using Demonstratives, Determiners, and Pronouns

USE

- You can use demonstrative determiners to refer to nouns that have been specified by **prior mention**. (See Unit 25)
  - **(a)** There once was **a** wicked king who lived in **a** castle. Every day **this king** would go to **a** secret room in **the** castle. **This** is where he liked to count his money. **It** was also the place where he kept his beautiful daughter.
- You do not usually repeat a demonstrative to refer to the same item. You should use a personal pronoun or a definite determiner instead.
  - **(b)** Have you tried **these** pears? **They** are quite delicious.
  - **(c)** NOT: Have you tried **these** pears? **These** are quite delicious.
  - **(d)** **This** is the problem Denise was talking about. **It** will continue to get worse, if we don't find a solution.
  - **(e)** NOT: **This** is the problem Denise was talking about. **This** will continue to get worse if we don't find a solution.
  - **(f)** I bought **that** pen and **this** notebook at a drugstore. **The** pen was a little expensive, but **the** notebook was cheap.
  - **(g)** NOT: I bought **that** pen and **this** notebook at the drugstore. **That** pen was a little expensive, but **this** notebook was cheap.

  - When you use two demonstratives, they must refer to different items.
    - **(h)** I don't like **these pears**, but **those** (different pears) are delicious.

Exercise 1

Add appropriate demonstratives, pronouns, and determiners to the blanks provided. More than one answer may be possible. The first one has been done for you as an example.

1. When Denise came to Mr. Green with her complaints about Peter, he realized that

   they had talked about ____*these*____ issues before. He told her there was no point in

   discussing ____*them*____ any further.

2. I got these new skirts and blouses on sale. I'd like you to take a look at _____ .

   Which of _____ dresses do you like better, _____ red one or _____

   green one? What about _____ blouses? Which do you prefer? _____ one

   or _____ one?

3. I got a new bike for my birthday. _____ was a gift from my parents. I'm glad they got _____ bike instead of another kind. _____ will be much more practical.

4. The essay that John wrote didn't receive a passing grade. _____ didn't contain any of the guidelines Dr. Montaigne had explained when she had first assigned _____ essay. _____ guidelines were not simple, but _____ had to be followed in order to get a passing grade on _____ essay. _____ grade made John rather upset, but Dr. Montaigne had made _____ guidelines quite clear.

5. Where did you get _____ ring? _____ is really beautiful. _____ looks like _____ came from Mexico. Is _____ silver?

Focus 3

Demonstratives for Reference

MEANING

- One very common use of demonstratives is to refer to information in previous sentences. There are two kinds of reference:
  - backward-pointing reference:
    (a) Everyone started laughing. **This** made John very angry.
    (b) I knew it was going to rain! **That's** why I didn't want to come to this picnic in the first place.
  - forward-pointing reference:
    (c) **This** is why I can't come to your party: I don't have the time, I don't have the clothes, and I have no way to get there.
    (d) I like **these** kinds of Asian food: Chinese, Japanese, Indian, and Thai.
- Using a particular form depends on whether it refers forward or backward in the text:
  - *This and these* can be used to point both forward or backward.
  - *That and those* can only be used for backward-pointing reference (except with postmodifiers—see Focus 5).
  - Pronouns (such as **it**) almost always refer back to previous elements in a text.

Exercise 2

What do the demonstratives refer to in these sentences? Circle the demonstratives in these passages. Then draw an arrow to what each one refers to. Is it an example of forward-pointing or backward-pointing reference? The first passage has been done for you as an example.

1. Most people find it difficult to sleep during the day and work at night. **This** is why people who work "swing shift" (as **that** work schedule is called) are usually paid a higher wage than **those** who work during the day.

2. We hold these truths to be self-evident, that all men are created equal and have a right to life, liberty, and the pursuit of happiness.

3. Let me make this perfectly clear: No new taxes!

4. Frank said that he wanted to leave New York because he was tired of big city life. But I don't think that was the real reason for his move to California. The real reason was that his wife wanted to live in a place with warmer winters. At least, this is what Stuart told me.

5. These soldiers must report immediately to Barracks B: Adams, Collins, and Powell. These men have been assigned to patrol duty: Westmoreland and MacArthur. Those are your orders, men. Troops dismissed!

6. The causes of the American Civil War were not substantially different from those of other wars that have taken place between different regions of any country. This is one of the things that can be learned by studying history.

7. The chemical properties of baking soda are similar to those of any base. This is what allows baking soda to enter into a chemical reaction with any acid, such as that found in vinegar or even orange juice.

8. The management techniques of many American companies now tend to resemble those used in Japan much more closely than they did a few years ago. This is largely attributable to the undeniable success those techniques have had in raising worker productivity.

Focus 4

Using *This / That* versus *It*

USE

- Both demonstrative pronouns (***this / that***) and personal pronouns (***it***) refer back to ideas or items in previous sentences. There is a difference in emphasis.

	Implied Meaning
"Did you hear the news? Scott is in jail." **(a)** "I knew **it**! That boy was always a troublemaker!	I'm not surprised!
(b) "I knew **that**. His mother told me last week."	I'd already heard that news.

- Using ***this/that*** emphasizes that the idea it refers to is the most important information in the new sentence:

> They say that *Mary is getting married to Paul.*
> **(c)** Does John know **that**?
> **(d)** Has John heard about **this**?

- Using **it** indicates some reaction to the idea on the part of the speaker.

They say that *Mary is getting married to Paul.* **(e)** I don't believe **it**! **(f)** I never would have suspected **it**.	***It*** indicates that our emphasis is on the verb—*believing* or *suspecting*.

- In some cases, you **must** use ***that*** instead of ***it***. This is especially true in cases where ***it*** could refer to a physical object rather than an abstract idea or situation.

(g) Don't leave your keys in the car. Someone might steal **it**. **(h)** Don't worry. I'm smarter than **that**.	NOT: Don't worry. I'm smarter than **it**. (This sounds like we are referring to the car.)
Aunt Martha is planning to bring her dog when she visits us. **(i)** I was afraid of **that**! No wonder she was asking if we had cats.	(***That*** indicates we are referring to the situation, not the dog.)

Exercise 3

Choose **this**, **that**, or **it** to put in the blanks of these sentences. Some sentences can use all three with little change of meaning. For some sentences, the choice might indicate a particular emphasis. For some sentences, one form may not be acceptable. Discuss your ideas with other students and your teacher.

1. Someone took your wallet? I was afraid _____ would happen. I told you not to leave your book bag in the library.

2. I'm glad Deborah hasn't had her baby yet. She was afraid _____ would happen while her husband was out of town.

3. I'm sorry you had to spend such a beautiful, sunny day in the library. _____ isn't really fair, is it?

4. I assume you have all heard the news about Arthur. _____ is why I have asked you to come to this meeting.

5. I love the wonderful California climate. _____ is why I moved here.

6. Did you say George's son is involved in another financial scandal? Are you sure of _____ ?

7. I just know Mary's dating someone else. I'm sure of _____ !

8. If you don't take advantage of this great opportunity, I know you'll regret _____ in the future.

9. Don't worry about making such a mess. _____ really doesn't matter.

10. Don't worry about making such a mess. _____ is why I put newspapers over everything.

11. You said "17." Don't you mean "70"? Oh yes, _____ 's what I meant.

12. Don't complain to me. _____ is why we have a complaint department.

Focus 5

That / Those with Forward-Pointing Reference

USE

- You can use *that* and *those* for forward-pointing reference only when they occur with
  - a relative clause:
    - **(a)** **Those who cannot learn from history** are doomed to repeat it.
    - **(b)** I'm not very fond of dogs, but **those that are well behaved** are OK.
    - **(c)** The boss only gives raises to **those** he really likes. (*whom* has been omitted)
    - **(d)** This script is really confusing. I can't tell the difference between **that which is supposed to be spoken** and **that which is supposed to be sung**.
  - a prepositional phrase:
    - **(e)** Compare your paragraph to **that of another student** in the class.
    - **(f)** This problem will have to be decided by **those in charge**.

Exercise 4

Identify the demonstratives that are followed by post-modifiers in these passages. Not all sentences contain this structure:

1. There is an old proverb that says God helps those that help themselves.
2. Please put those in the refrigerator.
3. My brother is very fussy about eating certain vegetables. He won't touch these, but those he likes won't stay on his plate for very long.
4. Those in the stock brokerage business think that this is a bad time to invest.
5. One must learn to distinguish between that which is necessary and that which is only desirable.
6. Those who can't tell the difference between teal and aquamarine shouldn't become interior decorators.
7. That is not my responsibility. You'll have to speak to those in charge of that part of the operations.
8. I read about that in the newspapers.

Focus 6

Special Uses of Demonstratives

- In very informal speech or written narratives, people sometimes use **this** and **these** in place of indefinite determiners to introduce nouns for the first time.
  - **(a)** I'm walking down the street, and I see **this** man on the corner. He's talking with **these** two other guys.
- Do not use **that** to refer to humans, except when you are pointing to the person.
  - **(b)** **That** man over there is married to **that** woman in the red dress.
  - When **that** is used in other kinds of reference, it usually indicates the speaker is annoyed, or is insulting the referent.
    - **(c)** Are you talking to **that** boy again? I told you not to speak to him!
    - **(d)** **That's** our brother! He's always trying to tell us younger kids what to do.
    - **(e)** I can't believe you're actually going to marry **that!** (This implies that the person being referred to is considered by the speaker to be a thing, rather than a human being.)

Answer to Activity 1:

That that is, is. That that is not, is not. Isn't it? It is!

Activities

Activity 1

Here is a puzzle. Can you punctuate this so that it makes sense?

that that is is that that is not is not isn't that it it is

There are four sentences in the correct answer, and that is printed upside down on the previous page.

Activity 2

Write a dialogue like the one in the Task. Work with a partner. First, decide what the argument will be about. Then write your dialogue. Try to use some of the phrases that Peter and Denise used.

• Perform your dialogue for the rest of the class.

Activity 3

Listen to an argument in a television comedy or drama. Write down any examples that you hear using *that* or *it*. Why do you think the speakers used a particular form?

Activity 4

Compare two products from different countries or people from two different settings. For example: How does the coffee of Guatemala differ from that of Sumatra? How do students in high school differ from those in college? Present your comparison in either written or spoken form.

Activity 5

Tell a story in informal spoken English. Use the Present Time Frame and demonstratives (*this* and *these*) instead of indefinite articles. See Focus 6 for an example to get you started.

27

Possessives

Task

What's wrong with this picture? How observant are you? There are at least 10 rather strange things about this picture. For example, the legs of the table seem to be a person's legs. The child's hair appears to be snakes. Find as many other strange things as you can and describe them.

Focus 1

Possessive Forms

FORM

- There are four kinds of possessive forms:
  - **Possessive determiners** (*my, your, his, her, its, our,* and *their*): Possessive determiners precede the noun.

    (a) Peter, John, and I left **our** shoes on the porch.
  - **Possessive pronouns** (*mine, yours, his, hers, its,* and *theirs*): Possessive pronouns can take the place of the noun phrase.

    (b) Mine were covered with mud.
  - **Possessive phrases** (Formed by adding the prepositional phrase *of*+**noun**): Possessive phrases follow the noun.

    (c) The steps **of the porch** looked like a meeting place for old, dirty shoes.
    the leg **of the chair**
    the end **of the story**
  - **Possessive nouns:** Formed by adding *'s* (pronounced **apostrophe-s**) to a noun, or simply adding an apostrophe to nouns ending in *-s*.

    (d) John's shoes were wet, and **Peter's** were greasy.
    the **student's** answers
    those **babies'** cries
    the **children's** laughter
    Phyllis' cousin

Exercise 1

Underline and identify all the possessive structures in the following passage. Are they *(a)* possessive determiners, *(b)* possessive pronouns, *(c)* possessive nouns, or *(d)* possessive phrases. The first paragraph has been done for you as an example.

Do all the identified structures describe possessive relationships?

(1)Have you ever tested your *(a)* memory? (2)There have been many studies of people's *(c)* ability to remember things. (3)These studies have found that there are two types of memory: *(d)* short-term memory and long-term memory.

(4)Short-term memory depends on the "length" or number of items that someone needs to remember. (5)A person's ability to remember a series of numbers for more than a minute is limited to about 12 or 14 digits. (6)An individual's ability to remember strings of unconnected words seems to average about eight items. (7)Most people's performance on such memory tests will drop quickly if they are tested again, even after only a few hours' time.

(8)Long-term memory seems to be determined by the item's usefulness to the person being tested. (9)For example, people do a better job of remembering one of Shakespeare's sonnets if they can apply the "message" of the poem to some part of their own lives. (10)The more important a piece of information is to a person's life, the longer and more accurately it can be retained.

Focus 2

USE

Possessive Nouns versus Possessive Phrases

USE

- Possessive nouns ('s) mean the same thing as nouns with a possessive prepositional phrase (*of...*), but there are guidelines for choosing one form over the other:
  (a) **The tall man's** face appeared in the window.
  (b) The face **of the tall man** appeared in the window.
- Most people prefer possessive nouns (with 's) for
  - most animate (living) things:

    the **boy's** cap   NOT: the cap **of the boy**
    the **horse's** mouth   NOT: the mouth **of the horse**
  - double possessives:

    Mary's mother's hat
    John's roommate's sweater
    the **President's secretary's** desk
  - objects that perform an action:
    the **razor's** edge
    the **train's** arrival
    the **rocket's** red glare
  - natural phenomena:
    the **moon's** orbit
    the **river's** mouth
    the **earth's** atmosphere

- Most people prefer possessive phrases (with *of* + noun phrase):
  - for most inanimate (nonliving) things:

    the back **of the chair**   NOT: the **chair's** back

    the roof **of the house**   NOT: the **house's** roof

    the cause **of the problem**   NOT: the **problem's** cause

  - when a possessive noun phrase is very long:

    the daughter **of a well-known local politician**

    NOT: **a well-known local politician's** daughter

  - when a multiple possessive is long:

    the hat of Mary's little, old-fashioned mother

    NOT: **Mary's little, old-fashioned mother's hat**

Exercise 2

For each noun + possessive listed here, write the best possessive form in the blank in the sentence. Add articles where necessary.

  EXAMPLES: hat/boy: *The boy's hat* blew into the sea.

      cover/*Time Magazine*: Being on the cover of *Time Magazine* made Elvis Presley even more famous.

1. results/investigation: _____ were reported in the newspaper.

2. restaurant/Alice's mother: We had dinner at _____

3. ability/individual: _____ to remember something depends on how important the information is.

4. rights/women: Suffragettes were early activists in the battle for _____

5. first chapter/novel: _____ begins with the famous words, "Call me Ishmael."

6. take-off/rocket: _____ was quite an amazing spectacle.

7. music/Elvis Presley: _____ has been heard all over the world.

8. discovery/penicillin: Sir Alexander Fleming was responsible for _____

  _____.

9. children/a very famous American movie star: I went to school with _____

  _____.

10. rotation/earth _____ is what causes night and day.

Exercise 3

Make up five sentences of your own that use the 's possessive form or the *of* possessive form. Explain why you chose the form that you did.

Exercise 4

Change the cues in parentheses to the correct possessive constructions. Add articles where necessary.

Last week Matt went shopping. It was (1)_____ (his roommate Jeff/birthday), and he wanted to buy a really "unusual" gift. He drove (2)_____ (Jeff/car) downtown. When he got there, he realized that the (3)_____ (shopping district/center) was already quite crowded, and most of (4)_____ (stores/ parking lots) were already full. He was in a hurry, so he decided to park in front of a hotel. He thought the (5)_____ (hotel/doorman) looked annoyed, but he was not paying attention. He visited several stores. In (6)_____ (one of the stores/window) he saw the perfect gift: a statue of a cowboy. In (7)_____ (cowboy/hand) there was a container for toothpaste, toothbrush, and a razor. He thought that the statue would look perfect in (8)_____ (their apartment/bathroom). He bought it and hurried back to where he had parked. The car was gone! At first, Matt thought it had been stolen, but then he realized that it had probably been towed away. He called the police, and they verified that the car was at the station. When he got there, he found that (9)_____ (car/front fender) had a dent, and there was a big scratch on (10)_____ (car/side). Matt had to pay for the (11)_____ (repair/cost) and the towing charges. Jeff got a very expensive birthday present, and Matt got a long-overdue lesson about traffic laws and parking regulations.

357

Exercise 5

Find out some information about the opinions of a classmate on these topics, and his or her reasons for those opinions. Ask questions that determine information about the following things. Report your partner's answers to the rest of the class.

> **EXAMPLE:** best place to sit in a classroom
>
> *You: What's the best place to sit in a classroom.*
>
> *Your partner: The front of the class is better if you're a good student, but the back of the class is better if you want to sleep.*

1. most important part of the semester (beginning, end, or middle)
2. favorite object that belongs to someone else
3. most important period of history
4. favorite piece of music

Ask two questions of your own that use possessive forms.

Focus 3

MEANING

Other Meanings of Possessive Forms

MEANING

- You can use possessive forms for other kinds of meaning besides **belonging to** someone or something. You can also use possessive forms to indicate
  - amount or quantity:
    - **(a)** Please give me three **dollars'** worth of unleaded gasoline.
    - **(b)** That leather coat cost me a **week's** pay.
    - **(c)** This book represents three **years'** work.
  - part of a whole:
    - **(d)** A **book's index** is a useful place to start when you're looking for specific information.
    - **(e)** John is the most dependable **of all my friends**.
  - a general relationship or association:
    - **(f)** Scientists are still trying to discover **the cause of cancer**.
    - **(g)** **The streets of New York** can be dangerous at night.
  - origin or agent:
    - **(h)** We studied **the sonnets of Shakespeare** in high school.
    - **(i)** **Joan's conversation** with the doctor caused her some concern.
  - identifying a topic:
    - **(j)** *Of Mice and Men* and *Of Human Bondage* are two famous twentieth-century novels.
    - **(k)** He told us **of his experiences in the army**.

Exercise 6

Underline the possessive forms in the following sentences and identify their meaning. Do they indicate

(a) an amount or quantity
(b) a part of a whole
(c) a general relationship/association
(d) an origin or agent
(e) an identified topic
(f) actual possession

                                        (b)   *(b)*

EXAMPLE: <u>The streets of San Francisco</u> are famous for <u>their steep hills</u>.

1. Scientists are studying the effects of alcohol on an individual's memory.

2. The wines of France are among the best in the world.

3. The teacher's assistant will hand back the homework.

4. That concept was introduced in the book's first chapter.

5. Chicago is four days' drive from Los Angeles.

6. An investigation of short-term memory has shown that items of personal importance are more easily remembered.

7. The steps of the porch looked like a meeting place of old, dirty shoes.

8. Matt's roommate likes ice cream.

9. Beethoven's symphonies are still thrilling.

Exercise 7

Read the following passage and underline all the possessive structures.

- For each possessive structure you identify, decide on the actual meaning indicated. Mark each structure with a letter to indicate whether the meaning is

(a) an amount or quantity	**(d)** an origin or agent
(b) a part of a whole	**(e)** an identified topic
(c) a general relationship/association	**(f)** actual possession

- Are there other phrases with *of* that are not possessive structures? Mark those structures with an X.

- For each possessive noun or possessive phrase you identify, explain why you think the author chose that form instead of another. The first paragraph has been done for you as an example.

(1)The most-visited residence in the United States is, *of course* (x), the White House, in Washington, DC, the home *of the President* (f) *of the United States* (c). (2)But the second most-visited residence may surprise you. (3)It is Graceland Mansion in Memphis, Tennessee, the home *of Elvis Presley* (f), the "King" *of rock and roll* (e). (4)Presley's influence on the popular music of America was profound. (5)He was one *of the first blues artists* (b) to make rock and roll popular with the middle class *of the United States* (b). (6)And *Elvis's* (f) swinging hips and sexy voice made him the dream boyfriend *of an entire generation* (f) *of teenage girls* (b).

(7)Presley's historic appearance on a 1958 broadcast of the "Ed Sullivan Show" caused an uproar. (8)His singing could not be heard because of the screams of his adoring fans. (9)And Presley's famous swinging hips were not seen at all, because of the objections of TV broadcasters, who felt his wild movements were not suitable for family television. (10)Presley rapidly became America's most popular male singer of all time. (11)He made hundreds of records and dozens of films. (12)Everywhere he went crowds of screaming, adoring fans showered him with gifts, love, and devotion.

(13)But his personal life was marked by tragedy. (14)By the time he died in 1977, everyone had heard the rumors of his troubles with alcohol and drugs. (15)They had read of his failed marriage in the movie magazines. (16)His suspicions about his friends' loyalties and motivations had made a "living nightmare" of his life. (17)He died a prisoner of his own popularity.

(18)In spite of his death, Elvis is still called The King of Rock and Roll. (19)Graceland Mansion is visited by hundreds of adoring fans every day. (20)His records continue to be popular, and there are several radio stations that play nothing but Presley's music.

(21)Some people even believe that he is still alive and living in disguise. (22)There continue to be rumors that his mysterious death was just a trick to allow him to escape from the prison of his fame and his fans' adoration. (23)Many people still believe that he is living a quiet life with a new name and a thick beard to hide his famous face. (24)Today the Memphis post office still receives hundreds of letters addressed to Elvis at Graceland from fans who still await "The King's" return.

Exercise 8

Are the following sentences correct or incorrect? If they are incorrect, identify the problem and correct it.

1. The fame of Elvis Presley spread across America.
2. The table's top was covered with newspapers.
3. The child of Bambang's classmate was sick with the flu.
4. Gladys' well-known next-door neighbor's dog's barking annoyed the entire neighborhood.
5. The scientists' studies' results indicate that memory is affected by such things as weather and time of day.
6. Memory's investigations have shown that the ability of people to remember things declines with age.
7. Rock and roll's king died in 1977.
8. Elvis' death's circumstances are somewhat mysterious.

Activities

Activity 1

Work with a partner to fill in the missing parts of these diagrams. Diagram A contains elements not contained in Diagram B (on the next page). Help your partner complete diagram B correctly. Your partner should help you complete Diagram C, which is incomplete. You should not look at Diagrams B and D. Your partner should not look at Diagrams A and C.

Diagram A (complete)   **Diagram C (incomplete)**

Activity 2

Write a short description of a famous person. What are the things that made him or her famous? Here are some things you might mention in your description: his or her accomplishments, childhood, important experiences, and influence on society.

Activity 3

Check your short-term memory. Study the picture at the beginning of this chapter for 30 seconds. Then close your book and describe it to a partner. Your partner should look at the picture while you describe it and check your description for accuracy.

Activity 1 (Diagrams B and D)

Diagram B (incomplete)   **Diagram D (complete)**

Activity 4

Oh, no! There's been an automobile accident! Look at the picture and describe what has happened to the car and its passengers. After you write your description, check the accuracy of your use of possessive forms.

28

Quantifiers

Task

Each year the Institute for International Education publishes a statistical profile on international educational exchange. They provide enrollment figures for students who go to another country to study. Examine the following charts on the enrollment of foreign students in educational institutions in the United States.

- Using the information in those charts and your own knowledge, write a brief essay on foreign students in the United States. Talk about general trends and possible exceptions to those trends. Provide information that answers these three questions:

What fields of study do international students pursue in the United States?
How do they finance their education?
Where do most students study?

A. Foreign Students by Field of Study, 1989/90

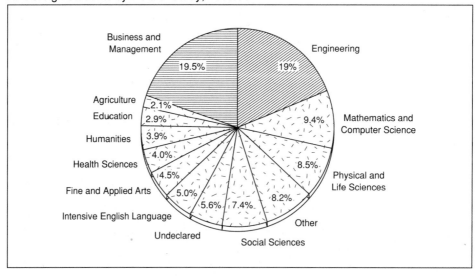

B. Foreign Students by Primary Sources of Funds, 1989/90

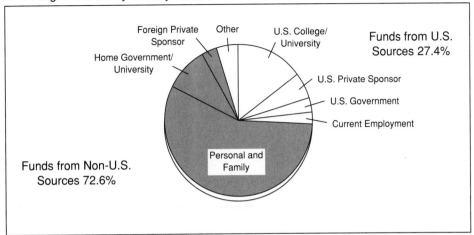

Foreign Private Sponsor

Other

U.S. College/ University

Funds from U.S. Sources 27.4%

Home Government/ University

U.S. Private Sponsor

U.S. Government

Current Employment

Personal and Family

Funds from Non-U.S. Sources 72.6%

C. Foreign Student Enrollment by U.S. State, 1989/90

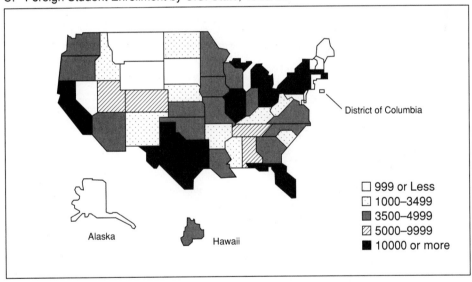

District of Columbia

Alaska

Hawaii

☐ 999 or Less
☐ 1000–3499
■ 3500–4999
▨ 5000–9999
■ 10000 or more

365

MEANING
Quantifiers in English

MEANING

- You can use quantifiers with noun phrases to describe **number** (with count nouns) or **amount** (with non-count nouns). There are two kinds of quantifiers: affirmative quantifiers and negative quantifiers. We have listed quantifiers and phrases with similar meaning in this chart in decreasing order from **all** (100 percent) to **none** (0 percent).

Quantifiers		Phrases of Quantity and Amount With Similar Meaning
Affirmative Quantifiers		
Used with Count Nouns	**Used with Non-Count Nouns**	
all/any *each/every*	*all/any*	*the total number/amount* *the entirety*
almost all	*almost all*	*the vast majority*
most	*most*	*the majority*
a great many *many* *lots of/a lot of* *plenty of*	*a great deal of* *much* *lots of/a lot of* *plenty of*	*a large number/amount*
a good number of	*a good deal of*	*more than some*
quite a few *quite a number of*	*quite a little* *quite a bit of*	*more than a few/a little*
some/any *several* *a (certain/large/small) number of*	*some/any* *a (certain/large/small) amount of*	*an indeterminate number/amount*
a few	*a little*	*a small number/amount*
Negative Quantifiers		
Used With Count Nouns	**Used With Non-Count Nouns**	
not all/not every	*not all*	*an unspecified number are/do not*
not many	*not much*	*a small number/amount*
few	*little*	*an insufficient number/amount*
hardly any *almost no/none*	*hardly any* *almost no/none*	*the vast majority are/do not*
no/none/not any	*no/none/not any*	*the total number/ amount are/do not*

Exercise 1

(a) In the following passage, underline the quantifiers and the noun phrases they modify. The first sentence has been done for you as an example.

(b) Are there quantifiers that do not appear with noun phrases? What sentences do they appear in and what do they refer to?

> **EXAMPLE:** *Clause 1 of the first sentence has a quantifier that does not appear with a noun phrase: many. It refers to* **people** *or* **experts.**

MEDICAL EDUCATION IN THE UNITED STATES

(1)Even though American medical education is considered by many to be the best in the world, (2)there are relatively few spaces in American medical schools, and a substantial number of Americans are forced to go overseas to get their basic medical training. (3)As a result, not all the doctors practicing in the United States have received their training from American medical schools. (4)In fact, quite a few have been educated in other countries. (5)However, all physicians must have clinical experience and pass qualifying examinations in order to receive a license to practice in the United States.

(6)Most doctors currently practicing in the United States have completed their practical training in an American hospital or clinic. (7)Every hospital in this country accepts a few recently graduated medical students each year, (8)including graduates from many foreign medical schools. (9)While some popular hospitals receive a great many applications for each available space, (10)a number of hospitals in rural areas may receive only a few. (11)This period of practical training is called a residency, and most last for two years. (12)A few are longer; some are shorter, depending on the specialization of the doctor.

(13)Many doctors study for an extra year before they begin their residency in order to become a specialist in a particular area of medicine. (14)No doctor is an expert in every area of medicine, but some doctors have more than one specialty. (15)Each area of medicine has its own period of residency and its own qualifying examinations.

Exercise 2

Write sentences that describe the training of medical doctors in another country that you are familiar with.

In (country),

1. Most doctors . . . .
2. Not all doctors . . . .
3. All doctors . . . .
4. A few doctors . . . .
5. No doctors . . . .
6. Many doctors . . . .

Focus 2

Affirmative Quantifiers

MEANING
USE

- You can use most affirmative quantifiers in both affirmative and negative statements and questions.

    (a) Do most foreign students have similar educational backgrounds?

    (b) Most graduate schools in the United States **require** an American B.A. degree.

    (c) Most foreign-trained medical students **don't have** clinical experience.

- But some affirmative quantifiers have special meanings or uses.
    - *All* and *almost all:*

(d) Not all graduate students have graduated from American universities. **(e)** AWKWARD: **All** graduate students **haven't** graduated from American universities. **(f)** NOT: **Almost all** graduate students **haven't** graduated from foreign institutions.	Generally *all* and *almost all* do not occur in negative sentences. It is more common to use the negative quantifier *not all* to express those ideas.

- *Any* has two possible meanings.

Some	
(g) Do you have **any** money? **(h)** She doesn't have **any** friends. **(i)** NOT: We ate **any** cookies.	This meaning of *any* is used with plural count nouns and non-count nouns. It is used in questions and negative statements but not in affirmative sentences.
All	
(j) Any American college requires students to be fluent in English.	This meaning of *any* is used with singular count nouns in affirmative sentences, but *any* does **not** mean *all* in questions or negatives.

- *Some* has two possible meanings.

An Unspecified Amount	
(k) Do you want **some** cake? **(l)** I've got **some** questions. **(m)** I **don't** have **any** money. **(n)** NOT: I **don't** have **some** money.	This use occurs only in questions and affirmative statements. In negative statements, the quantifier *any* is used.
A Certain Group or Amount	
(o) Some students came on time, but most of them were late. **(p) Some** students don't like to speak in class.	This use occurs in both affirmative and negative sentences.

- *Much:*

(q) Much of the financial support for study in the United States comes from the students themselves. **(r)** Does it take **much** money to pay for a university education? **(s)** The average foreign student **doesn't have much** money.	**Much** is usually used with specified nouns phrases (noun phrases with *the*), questions, and negative statements.
(t) NOT: I'm having **much** trouble finding a school. **(u)** I'm having **a lot of** trouble finding a school. **(v)** I'm having **a great deal of** trouble finding a school.	*Much* is **not** used with nonspecific noun phrases (noun phrases with *a/an* or no article) in affirmative sentences. *A lot (lots) of* is usually preferred in conversation. *A great deal of, quite a bit of, etc.,* are more common in written contexts.

Exercise 3

Change the following statements concerning number or amount to sentences using quantifiers.

EXAMPLE: The vast majority of students pass their qualifying examination on the first try.

Almost all students pass the exams on their first try.

1. The vast majority of medical students in the United States already have B.A. degrees.
2. An indeterminate number of students have more than one major.
3. There are a small number of scholarships for international students.
4. It takes a large amount of money to fund a university education.
5. A small number of students apply to only one university for admission.
6. An unspecified number of applicants don't pass the qualifying exams such as TOEFL, GRE, or GMAT.
7. The majority of international students apply for admission to more than one university.
8. A large number of students study English before they begin their academic studies.

Exercise 4

What is wrong with these sentences?

1. All doctors don't apply to several hospitals for residency.
2. Some students don't have some trouble passing their exams.
3. Other students have any trouble, but usually pass on the second time.
4. A medical education requires much money.

Exercise 5

Make statements about the statistics you studied in the Task, using each of the quantifiers listed below.

EXAMPLE: *most—Most foreign students in the United States pay for their own education.*

1. all
2. a great many
3. quite a few
4. a lot of
5. a little
6. several

7. some
8. any
9. a few
10. a great deal of
11. much

Focus 3

MEANING ● USE

Negative Quantifiers

MEANING
USE

- Negative quantifiers have a negative meaning and usually do not occur in sentences with negative verbs.

(a) AWKWARD: **Few** doctors **don't** have medical degrees.

(b) BETTER: Almost all doctors have medical degrees.

(c) NOT: **Not all** students **don't** pass the TOEFL on their first try.

(d) BETTER: Some students pass the TOEFL on their first try.

(e) AWKWARD: **None** of the students **didn't** pass the qualifying exams.

(f) BETTER: All the students passed.

- Negative quantifiers often imply that the amount or number is insufficient:

Affirmative Quantifiers (A Small Amount)	Negative Quantifiers (Not Enough)
(g) A few doctors have studied nonwestern medicine. (**Some** doctors have studied it.) **(i)** There's **a little** money left after the bills are paid. (There is still **some** money for other things.)	**(h) Few** doctors have studied nonwestern medicine. (**An insufficient number** have studied it.) **(j)** There's **little** money left after the bills are paid. (There is **not enough** money for other things.)

370

Exercise 6

Decide whether to use *few* or *a few*, *little* or *a little*. Compare your answers to those of a partner. Prepare to explain why you chose your answer.

1. The students were discouraged because _____ people passed the examination.

2. Even the very best students have _____ difficulty gaining admission to a good university.

3. I can loan you some money, but I've only got _____ dollars.

4. They were working in the laboratory for so long that now there's _____ time to get ready for the quiz.

5. There are _____ scholarships available for first-year medical students, so a medical education is expensive.

6. He put _____ effort into studying for examinations, and as a result didn't pass on the first try.

7. The average medical student usually applies to at least _____ places for residency.

8. Bambang had _____ trouble finding a university. Several schools were willing to accept him.

Exercise 7

Using the following negative quantifiers, make true statements about the statistics on international education that you studied in the Task.

1. few
2. not all
3. little
4. hardly any
5. no

Focus 4

Each, Every, Any, No: Quantifiers Used with Singular Nouns

FORM

- Most quantifiers are used with plural count nouns and non-count nouns, but there are a few that are used with singular count nouns. Their meaning is the same as that of *all*.
  - *Each, every* and *any:*

(a) The teacher asked **each student** a question. (**All students** were asked.) **(b)** **Every student** wants to get an *A* in this class. (**All students** want *A*'s.) **(c)** **Any doctor** knows basic first aid techniques. (All doctors know basic first aid.)	These quantifiers are only used with singular count nouns. **Each** and **any** emphasize individual members of the group. **Every** emphasizes the group as a whole.

- *No:*

(d) **No student** has ever taken this test more than once. **(e)** **No doctors** in this country are allowed to practice without a license.	**No** can be used with both singular and plural nouns.

Exercise 8

Change the following statements with plural count nouns to statements with *any, each,* or *every*. Remember to make any other necessary changes to preserve the meaning of the original sentence. More than one answer may be correct, so prepare to explain why you chose the answer you did.

> **EXAMPLE:** All doctors know basic first aid.
> *Every doctor knows basic first aid.*
> *Any doctor knows basic first aid.*

1. All doctors must complete their residencies within two years.
2. All parents want their children to succeed in life.
3. Peter spends all free weekends at the beach.
4. All the people who came to the examination brought calculators.
5. A wise student takes advantage of all opportunities to gain practical experience.

Exercise 9

Complete the following sentences with true information:

1. Each student in this class . . . .
2. Every teacher I have had . . . .
3. Any English class . . . .
4. No student . . . .
5. No teachers . . . .

Focus 5

FORM ● MEANING

Both, Either, and Neither: Fixed-Number Quantifiers

FORM
MEANING

- You can use the quantifiers *both, either,* and *neither* only when you are talking about **two count nouns:**

Form	Meaning	Use
both	**two**	**(a)** Albert and Florence took their medical qualifying exams. **Both students** passed.
neither	**both do not**	**(b) Both** had worried about failing the exams, but **neither student** did.
either	**both** **one or the other**	**(c)** I would trust **either one** to do complex surgery. **(d)** But only one will get the residency. It will be **either** Albert **or** Florence, I'm sure.

- See Unit 8 for more information and practice with *both, either,* and *neither.*

Exercise 10

Here is some information about two medical students, Florence Schweitzer and Albert Nightingale:

Florence Schweitzer passed her qualifying exams last week. She has applied for a residency at Providence Hospital. Her specialization is orthopedics. She took the exams last year, but she didn't pass. Providence has only one residency available for this year, but Florence is optimistic. She got very high scores on her specialization exam, and her friend Albert is the only other person who has applied for a residency.

Albert Nightingale passed his qualifying exams last week. He also applied for a residency at Providence. His specialization is pediatrics. This was his second time taking the exams too. He has also applied to Mercy Hospital, and likes the training programs at both hospitals, so he doesn't care which hospital accepts him.

Use each of these quantifiers *(both, neither, either, both of them,* and *either of them)* in the following blanks so that the statements reflect this information.

1. _____ students took their qualifying exams.

2. _____ student passed the first time, but _____

   passed on the second try.

3. Albert will accept a residency at _____ hospital.

4. Albert has applied to two hospitals, and will accept a residency at _____

Exercise 11

Use the quantifiers in **Exercise 10** to make true statements about two students in your class.

Focus 6

Using Quantifiers with *Of*

FORM

- When using most quantifiers with specific noun phrases, (nouns that use a definite determiner such as **the, this,** or *his*) you must add the preposition **of**. Examine the differences in these two kinds of sentences.

Generic/Nonspecific Reference	Specific Reference
(a) Any bus will take you downtown.	**(b) Any of the buses** that stop here will take you downtown.
(c) Most students want to get good grades.	**(d) Most of the** students who Donna teaches have college degrees.
(e) Several cars have passed.	**(f) Several of the cars** at the police station had been stolen.
(g) Some students never study.	**(h) Some of the students** in this class didn't pass the exam.
(i) Few old-fashioned doctors realize the importance of exercise.	**(j) Few of the doctors** trained in recent years still smoke.
(k) There are **hardly any students** in class today.	**(l) Hardly any of the students** who took the exam yesterday came to school.
(m) I brought **a little wine** to the party.	**(n) A little of the wine** I bought is still left.
(o) Little money is being spent on child-care programs.	**(p) Little of the money** we collected from the book sale is left.
(q) Hardly any time is left to answer questions.	**(r) Hardly any of the time** we spent in class was used for review.

- See Unit 25 for more information and practice with specific and nonspecific nouns.

- **Special cases**
  - You can use **all** with or without *of* in specific reference:

Nonspecific Reference	Specific Reference
(s) All students hate to take tests.	**(t) All the students** in this class hate tests. **(u) All of the students** in this class hate tests.

  - You can use **no** and **almost no** only for nonspecific reference. You must use **none** with specific reference:

Nonspecific Reference	Specific Reference
(v) No buses run after midnight. **(x) Almost no information** was available from the office.	**(w) None of the buses** that run after midnight stop here. **(y) Almost none of the advice** he gave me was very practical.

Exercise 12

Decide whether to use a **quantifier** or **quantifier + of** for the following sentences:

1. (All) _____ laboratory equipment on this table should be sterilized before use.

2. (Any) _____ information you provided yesterday will be used to help others.

3. (Almost all) _____ plants require sunlight to survive.

4. (Most) _____ coffee served in restaurants contains caffeine.

5. You won't need (much) _____ your warm clothing if you go to medical school in the Philippines.

6. (A great deal) _____ the population still believes in traditional medicine.

7. (Some) _____ the information in your report was incomplete.

8. I don't need (any) _____ your help.

9. Bob wasted (little) _____ the money he won on frivolous things.

10. (No/None) _____ students came to the party.

Focus 7

Using Quantifiers in Place of Noun Phrases

USE

- You can use most quantifiers in place of nonspecific noun phrases if the meaning is clear.
  - **(a)** **Many American doctors** have studied acupuncture, but only **a few** actually practice it.
  - **(b)** **Some Western doctors** have been trained in non-Western medicine, but **most** haven't.
  - **(c)** Did **any candidates** fail the qualifying examinations? Yes, **lots.**
  - **(d)** Did Albert have **much trouble** with his car? **Quite a bit.**
- There are certain quantifiers that you cannot use to replace noun phrases:
  - *Much* and *many*:

(e) How much money have you got? I don't have **much.** How about you? **Not much.** We'd better stop at the bank and get a little. Are there any banks around here? **Not many.** I guess we'll have to go downtown.	These forms can only replace nouns in negative sentences, or when used with **not**.

  - *No:*

(f) Is it true that **no students** failed the test? That's correct. **None** did.	*No* cannot be used in place of a noun. *None* is used instead.

  - *Each/every:*

(g) Did **every** candidate pass the exam? Yes, **every one** of them did. NOT: Yes, **every** did.	*Each* and *every* cannot be used to replace a noun phrase. They must be used with *one*.

Exercise 13

Answer the following questions with complete sentences, using quantifiers in place of noun phrases.

EXAMPLE: Where are most doctors trained?

Most *are trained here in America, but* **some** *study medicine overseas.*

1. Do all doctors in the United States have to pass qualifying examinations?
2. How many candidates pass the exams on the first try?
3. How many American doctors are well-trained in non–Western medicine?
4. How much money does it take to get a medical education in the United States?
5. How much competition is there for admission to American medical schools?
6. How many doctors have basic training in first aid procedures?
7. How many residency positions do most medical students apply for?
8. How many Americans study at medical schools overseas?
9. How many foreign students are enrolled in United States medical schools?
10. How much persistence does it take to become a doctor in the United States?

Exercise 14

Choose the correct form in these sentences:

1. We don't need (some/any/none of) assistance with our baggage.
2. I feel sorry for Albert. He's so shy, and he has (few/a few/quite a few) friends he can talk to if he has problems.
3. Hardly any people (came/didn't come) to the meeting.
4. Albert went to (quite a bit of/a bit of/only a bit of) trouble to get those tickets, so you must remember to thank him.
5. (Not every/Not all/None of)people like to go dancing on Saturday nights.
6. Do you have (many/much/every) time to help me?
7. Sure I do. I've got (a lot/ lots of).
8. Why are Albert and Florence so sad? (Both/Neither/None) passed the chemistry exam.
9. Learning English takes (several/a certain amount of/any) practice.
10. (A great many of/ A great much of/ A great deal of) the time we spent in Hawaii, it was raining.

Exercise 15

Are the following sentences correct or incorrect? If they are incorrect, identify the problem and correct the sentence. There may be more than one problem.

1. None of doctors are allowed to practice without a license.
2. We had much trouble with the examination this morning.
3. A great many of traditional medicines are still used in rural areas.
4. No unlicensed physicians are allowed to practice in the United States.
5. Foreign students need lots of opportunities to get used to American educational techniques.
6. Few students never pass their qualifying exams.
7. Quite a bit of time that Albert spent in his residency was clinical training.
8. Students usually apply to several of universities for admission.
9. A few doctors don't stay up-to-date, but a lot of do.
10. Few students don't take their studies seriously.

Activities

Activity 1

In the Task, you examined some graphs on foreign student enrollment in the United States. Following is some information about foreign student enrollment patterns worldwide. Examine these two graphs and write a brief essay on foreign study throughout the world. Be sure to answer these questions:

- Where do students come from?
- Where do they go?
- What countries have the largest percentage of foreign students in their schools?

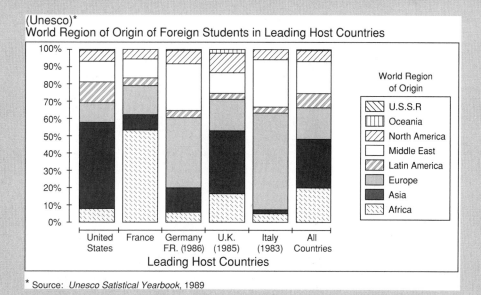

(Unesco)*
World Region of Origin of Foreign Students in Leading Host Countries

* Source: *Unesco Satistical Yearbook*, 1989

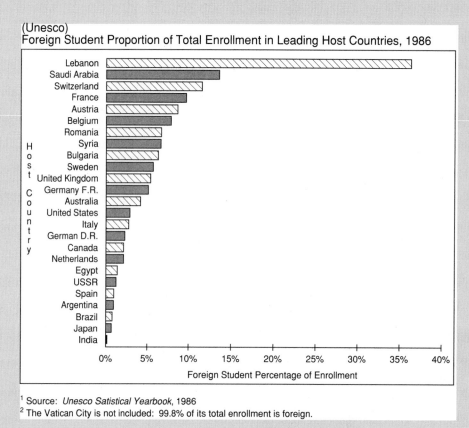

(Unesco)
Foreign Student Proportion of Total Enrollment in Leading Host Countries, 1986

Host Country (vertical axis labels, top to bottom):
Lebanon, Saudi Arabia, Switzerland, France, Austria, Belgium, Romania, Syria, Bulgaria, Sweden, United Kingdom, Germany F.R., Australia, United States, Italy, German D.R., Canada, Netherlands, Egypt, USSR, Spain, Argentina, Brazil, Japan, India

Horizontal axis: 0% 5% 10% 15% 20% 25% 30% 35% 40%
Foreign Student Percentage of Enrollment

[1] Source: *Unesco Satistical Yearbook*, 1986
[2] The Vatican City is not included: 99.8% of its total enrollment is foreign.

Activity 2

Conduct a poll of your classmates to find out about their educational backgrounds.

How many years of school do they have?
What subjects have they studied?
Did most of them enjoy school?
Decide on two more questions to ask them.

• Present your information by constructing charts similar to the ones you have been examining in this unit.

Activity 3

In **Exercise 1**, you read about the training of medical doctors in the United States. Describe how people in one of these categories are trained:

traditional artists	farmers	athletes
lawyers	plumbers	English teachers

Activity 4

Conduct a public opinion poll on some aspect of current events.

- In a group, choose some topic of current interest from the news and develop a list of 5–8 questions to determine how people feel about this issue.
- Poll your classmates, and also interview 10–15 people outside of class.
- Devise a graphic representation of your results similar to the charts you have examined in this unit.
- Using your charts, make a presentation of your findings to the rest of the class. Report any interesting differences between the opinions of your classmates and the people you interviewed outside of class.

Activity 5

President Abraham Lincoln was famous for this remark:

"You can fool all of the people some of the time, and you can fool some of the people all of the time. But you can't fool all of the people all of the time."

- Do you think this is true? Think of some examples that support your opinion and explain those examples in a short essay or speech to the rest of the class.

29

Collective Nouns

Task

What is a good way to organize a complicated group project? Business managers have found that certain organizational techniques can make any group or committee run more smoothly and efficiently. Bad organization can result in a few people doing all the work, duplication of effort, or wasted time and energy.

Here is an opportunity for you to explore techniques for streamlining group processes and decision making: Suppose the whole class has decided to take a weekend trip together. In a small group, decide on the best way to organize such a complex project to make sure that work is done efficiently and everyone is involved in the process.

- Decide on the **tasks** that need to be done in order to organize and carry out such a trip.
- Establish a list of **committees** to accomplish these tasks and specify the duties and members of each committee. Make sure that the work is evenly distributed, and that no single committee has too much to do.

When you have decided on your organizational plan, make a report to the rest of the class:

- Describe your organizational plan. Tell what committees you have established, what responsibilities each committee has, and who each committee has as members.
- Report on the decision-making process of your group. Identify any problems you had working as a committee. Present any techniques you used that helped you work together more efficiently.

The class should decide who has the best-organized plan for the project.

Focus 1

Collective Nouns

FORM

- There are two kinds of collective nouns: those that refer to groups of things and those that refer to categories. There are some differences in their form and use.
- Some collective nouns refer to groups of things. You can use them to describe groups of collections of

People	Animals	Things
a **troupe** of dancers	a **flock** of birds	a **bunch** of grapes
a **team** of ball players	a **herd** of goats	a **sheaf** of papers
a **committee** of experts	a **pack** of dogs	a **bundle** of letters
a **delegation** of officials	a **gaggle** of geese	a **group** of issues
a **coven** of witches	a **school** of fish	a **flurry** of new developments
	a **swarm** of insects	

- These collective nouns function like other count nouns. You can use them with or without the accompanying noun phrase. They can have both singular or plural forms:
  - **(a)** The **delegation of teachers** left the room.
  - **(b)** The **delegation** left the room.
  - **(c)** The president met with **several delegations** last week.
- The second group of collective nouns refer to categories. These categories are usually social or political categories:

the government	the administration
the middle class	the aristocracy
the media	the clergy
the bourgeoisie	the establishment
the public	the military-industrial complex
the opposition	the arts community

- These collective nouns that refer to categories function differently from collective nouns that refer to groups of things. They always occur with *the*. Their grammatical form is almost always singular.

  NOT: **a** clergy, **a** public, etc.

  NOT: the **publics** of the United States

Exercise 1

Read the following passages. Underline the words and phrases that refer to groups or categories of nouns. The first passage has been done for you as an example.

1. Every year on March 19, <u>a large flock of swallows</u> returns to San Juan Capistrano Mission in Southern California. No one knows how <u>this flock</u> manages to return every year on exactly the same date, but they have been doing just that for more than 200 years. <u>The Chamber of Commerce</u> in San Juan Capistrano has been providing mountains of publicity on the event for many years, and as a result, March 19 is also the day when <u>flocks of tourists</u> arrive at the Mission as well to watch the swallows return.

2. The World Cup Soccer Competition is probably the single most popular athletic event in the world. Teams of athletes from almost every country in the world conduct play-off matches. A team's standing depends on whether it has won or lost the previous game. A team that succeeds in reaching the finals can count on its fans to provide vigorous and energetic support. The young, the enthusiastic, and the dedicated invariably accompany them to the final round of play-offs and cheer them to victory.

3. A committee of scientists has been appointed by the government to look into the effects of acid rain on the forests of North America. They have been asked to present the results of their study to the President by the end of the year. The press and the public will be waiting anxiously for the committee to release its report.

4. There is a very unusual company of actors, which is based in Washington, D.C. Most of the company cannot hear, and many members can only speak by using sign language. The National Theater of the Deaf was founded nearly 30 years ago, and since then they have performed all over the United States and in dozens of foreign countries. The troupe has played an important role in involving the disabled in the arts.

Focus 2

FORM ● MEANING ● USE

Singular and Plural Meaning of Collective Nouns

FORM
MEANING
USE

- Collective nouns can have a singular or plural meaning. You can use them with either singular or plural verbs and pronouns.

(a) The committee of experts **has** decided to release **its** findings next week.	**(b) The committee** of experts **have** decided to release **their** findings next week.
(c) The aristocracy has opposed every challenge to **its** economic privileges.	**(d) The aristocracy have** opposed every challenge to **their** economic privileges.
(e) The middle class in America **has** begun to protest the accelerating decline in **its** standard of living.	**(f) The middle class** in America **have** begun to protest the accelerating decline in **their** standard of living.

- There is a difference in implication. Using singular verbs and pronouns usually implies that the group is operating as a whole. Using plural verbs and pronouns focuses on the individual behavior of the members of the group.

(g) The team **has** just won **its** third championship in a row.	**(h)** The team **are** entering the stadium, waving **their** hands and smiling at the crowd.

- There is also a difference in British and American usage. British English tends to use plural forms with singular collective nouns. American English tends to use singular forms with singular collective nouns:

British Usage	American Usage
(i) The committee **have** made **their** decision	**(j)** The committee **has** made **its** decision.
(k) The aristocracy **were** sometimes cruel to **their** servants.	**(l)** The aristocracy **was** despised for **its** lack of concern for the poor.

- Whichever choice you make, it is usually bad style in written or formal spoken English to change from singular to plural within a single sentence or single reference:

Singular	Plural
(m) The beginning class **likes its** teachers to give **it** lots of homework. **(o)** NOT: The beginning class **likes their** teachers to give **them** lots of homework.	**(n)** The beginning class **like their** teachers to give **them** lots of homework.

Exercise 2

Read the following sentences and underline each collective noun and any pronouns and verbs which refer to it. Decide why the author chose to consider the collective noun singular or plural.

> **EXAMPLE:** The French Revolution was caused in part by the refusal of the aristocracy to give up its social privileges.
>
> Reason: Reference to a single social class, not a collection of individuals.

1. The Roman Catholic clergy will resist any attempt to change its position on abortion.
2. The victorious team all waved to their supporters while the crowd roared its approval.
3. The media is aware of the important role it plays in American Presidential elections.
4. The herd of sheep bleated nervously to their shepherd as a pack of wolves made its way through the forest.
5. The military continues to fight further reductions in its funding.
6. The middle class is facing a greater tax burden than it has ever faced before.
7. A rash of new developments have made a great change on the government's priorities, and it is just beginning to respond to them.

Exercise 3

Decide whether you should use the collective nouns in the following sentences with singular or plural verbs and pronouns and choose the correct form. Although both choices may be grammatical, there may be a clear preference for one form instead of the other, so prepare to explain why you have chosen the forms you did.

1. The staff took a vote on what kind of Christmas party (it/they) (want/wants). (It/They) decided to rent a hall and hire a band.
2. The college administration (want/wants) a basketball team that (is/are) able to win enough games to place (itself/themselves) in the final play-offs.
3. The rowing crew raised (its/their) oars as (its/their) boat crossed the finish line.
4. The advanced grammar class never (like/likes) to turn in (its/their) homework right after a long vacation. (It/They) prefer to finish all assignments before (it/they) leave for vacation.
5. The crowd showed (its/their) approval by letting out a deafening roar.
6. The opposition voiced (its/their) disapproval to the policies the government had released in (its/their) latest report by more than three dozen speeches in Parliament.

Focus 3

MEANING

Singular and Plural Proper Nouns

MEANING

- Many singular proper nouns also describe groups. Most names of such things as organizations and legislative bodies are singular and should be used with singular verbs and pronouns:
    (a) The Supreme Court **has** changed **its** position on several issues.
    (b) The Congress of Deputies **has** requested the release of five political prisoners.
    (c) Parliament **has** adjourned for the summer.
    (d) The House of Representatives **has** begun debate on whether or not to raise the salaries of **its** members.
- Plural proper nouns refer to groups as a whole. Most names of nationalities, families, teams, and so on, are plural and should be used with plural verbs and pronouns:
    (e) **The Russians are** trying to transform **their** economy.
    (f) **The Montagues** and **the Capulets** were the two warring families in Shakespeare's *Romeo and Juliet*.
    (g) **The Democrats** hope to attract **their** supporters from the working class.
    (h) I hope **the Miami Dolphins were** able to win the game yesterday.

Exercise 4

Decide whether the following proper nouns should be considered singular or plural. Write a sentence for each. Be sure the verbs and pronouns in your sentences reflect your choice of whether these proper nouns are singular or plural.

1. The National Assembly
2. The French
3. The Russians
4. The Washington Redskins
5. The government of Brazil
6. The Catholic Church
7. The Chinese
8. The Grateful Dead
9. The Smith Family
10. The Simpsons

Focus 4

FORM ● MEANING

Adjectives Referring to Groups

FORM
MEANING

- Adjectives used with *the* can also refer to a group whose members share a particular characteristic. These constructions are considered to be plural, and the verbs and pronouns reflect this.
  - **(a) The rich** get richer and **the poor** get poorer.
  - **(b)** These laws are designed to protect **the young** and **the helpless** from exploitation.
  - **(c) The elderly are** making **their** opinions a growing force in American politics.

Exercise 5

For each *the* + **adjective** construction in the following sentences, rewrite the construction as **noun + relative clause**.

> **EXAMPLE:** The French aristocracy did not care about the poor.
>
> *The poor = people who were poor.*

1. Elvis Presley was very popular with the young.
2. *Dear Abby* is an advice column in the newspaper for the lonely and the confused.
3. Nelson Mandela is an important hero for the oppressed.
4. Albert and Florence became doctors so they could help the sick.
5. The government should establish more comprehensive programs to help the underprivileged.

Exercise 6

Circle the collective nouns, proper nouns, and adjectives that refer to groups in the following passage. Decide whether the pronouns and verbs that refer to these constructions should be singular or plural.

(1)The homeless *are/is* an increasing problem in most American cities. (2)The homeless *consist/consists* of several distinct categories of people. (3)The first category *consist/consists* of the mentally disabled. (4)In the early 1980s, the Reagan Administration eliminated most of *its/their* funding for treatment programs for the mentally ill. (5)As a result, scores of mental hospitals were closed, and many of the mentally ill *was/were* released, and left to make *its/their* own way. (6)A substantial number *have/has* been unable to establish normal lives, and as a result, *it/they* have ended up living on the streets.

(7)A second category of the homeless *is/are* the unemployed. (8)Typically, the unemployed *is/are* part of the homeless for a relatively short period of time—usually less than a year. (9)Some of *it/them have/has* lost *its/their* jobs; or the factories where *it/they* worked were closed without warning. (10)As a result, *it/they* did not have enough money to pay rent. (11)Many of the unemployed *has/have* also ended up living on the streets or sleeping in *its/their* automobiles. (12)But the majority of the people in this category of the homeless *is/are* able to find housing again, once they have found other jobs.

(13)A third category of the homeless *is/are* the people who *is/are* addicted to drugs or alcohol. (14)Like the mentally ill, this category of homelessness *represent/represents* a persistent social problem. (15)The unemployed can hope for better times, and *is/are* usually able to escape from the terrible cycle of poverty and life on the streets, but the government *has/have* been very slow in committing *its/their* resources to any kind of comprehensive program to help the mentally disabled or the addicted work on *its/their* recovery.

Focus 5

USE

Implications of Collective Nouns

USE

- Like the measure words that you can only use with certain non-count nouns (an **ear** of corn, for example), many collective nouns that refer to groups usually belong only to one particular group. Sometimes a writer will use an inappropriate collective noun to indicate that one group has characteristics common to another group.

As we watched, **a gaggle of schoolgirls** made their way through the mall.	*Gaggle* is the collective noun used for a group of geese. This sentence implies that the girls' activity resembled that of geese in some way.
When the scientists in Antarctica began construction of the research station, they were constantly watched by **a delegation of penguins** which showed no fear of humans.	*Delegation* is the collective used for official groups of representatives or diplomats. This sentence implies that the penguins appeared rather formal and official.

Exercise 7

Read the following sentences. Identify the collective nouns. Discuss with a partner or a small group what the choice of collective nouns implies. Share your ideas with the rest of the class.

1. The mayor was followed by a pack of reporters demanding to know whether he was planning to resign.
2. When herds of tourists filled the gallery, John decided to see the exhibition at another time.
3. A flock of school children filled the air with shouting and laughter.
4. Out of the jungle came a troupe of monkeys which snatched up the food that had been prepared for the picnic.
5. As soon as he stepped out of the limousine, he was surrounded by a swarm of beggars asking for money.

Exercise 8

Are these sentences correct or incorrect? If they are incorrect, identify the problem and correct it.

1. The Supreme Court have decided to reverse its opinion on that issue.
2. I watched the flock of birds as it landed in the field across the road.
3. The rich is always trying to avoid giving its money to pay taxes.
4. The Kremlin are trying to restructure the economy of the USSR.
5. The herd of sheep was frightened by a pack of wolves, and it bleated nervously in their pen.

Activities

Activity 1

English used to have many different collective nouns to refer to specific animals. These nouns sometimes indicated some sort of quality or characteristic that these animals had.

a pride of lions
a parliament of owls
a pod of whales
an exaltation of larks
a charm of finches
a leap of leopards

We rarely use such collective words in modern English. But sometimes for humorous reasons, people will invent collective words to apply to a particular group of people. Here are some examples:

a sweep of cleaning ladies
a hustle of salesmen
a splash of swimmers

- Working with a partner, decide on some humorous collective terms for some of these categories of people:

flight attendants	kittens
lawyers	puppies
accountants	computer programmers
English teachers	real-estate salesmen
magicians	

Activity 2

Write a paragraph on one of these topics:

- Compare two athletic teams that play a sport you are familiar with. Why do you think one team is better than the other?
- Discuss one or more famous performing troupes (opera, drama, circus, orchestra). Why are they famous and do you feel that their reputation is justified?
- What lessons can the old teach the young? What lessons can the young teach the old?

Activity 3

There is a joke in American business circles that says, "A camel is a horse that was designed by a committee." Some management experts think that committees result in a better product than a single individual. Others feel that committees tend to be inefficient and badly organized.

- In the Task, you had a firsthand experience with working in a committee. Review your experience with that process. What were the advantages of having a group work together on a single task? What were the disadvantages? Based on your experience, identify the strengths and weaknesses of working on a committee.
- Present your ideas to the rest of the class as a list of **pros** and **cons**. For example, *Pro:* A committee is able to assign tasks to each member, so the work can be divided. *Con:* A committee does not reach decisions quickly, because each member has to agree about the issue before they can take action.
- How are you going to do this activity? By yourself or in a group?

Activity 4

Should the rich pay more taxes or higher penalties (for traffic tickets, for example) than the poor? Why do you think so? Discuss your ideas in a small group and present a report on your group's opinion to the rest of the class. Your report should use phrases like "Our group feels that . . . "

Activity 5

Have you ever seen a political demonstration? Where and when did it occur? What was the demonstration about? What did the crowd do? What did the police do? Write a description of what happened.

UNIT

30

Special Problems in Past Time Frame:
Choosing Adverbs versus Aspect Markers to Indicate Time Relationships

Task

There are certain events that are so important or surprising that they are literally un-forgettable. For example, most Americans who were born before 1955 can probably tell you **exactly** what they were doing on November 22, 1963—the day President John F. Kennedy was assassinated—even though that day was more than 25 years ago. It was a day that few people can forget. Anyone living in San Francisco on October 17, 1989, can tell you exactly what he or she was doing when the earthquake occurred at 5:08 P.M.

- Write a paragraph describing a time when you heard some shocking or memorable news or experienced some important event—a time that you will never forget. You can tell about a time when you heard about some important development in world events such as Indira Gandhi's assassination or the tearing down of the Berlin Wall. Or it could be something more personal, such as the day your mother told you that you were going to have a new baby brother or sister. Start your account with: "I will never forget the moment that...." Your description should include what you were doing at the time, what you had been doing, and how you reacted when you heard the news.

Here are two accounts to look at as examples:

EXAMPLE 1:

(1)I will never forget the moment I heard that John F. Kennedy had been assassinated. (2)I was a junior in high school. (3)I was studying in the school library at the time. (4)Ordinarily, I would have been in the music room practicing with the school orchestra. (5)(I used to play the violin when I was in high school.) (6)But our teacher was conducting a special rehearsal for the wind instruments. (7)All of the string players had been excused from the rehearsal, so I had been given a pass to go to the library and do some independent studying.

(8)The library door was open, and I heard a radio playing from one of the classrooms across the hall. (9)At first, I was annoyed by the noise. (10)I wondered why they were playing that radio so loud when people were trying to study. (11)Then all of a sudden, I heard the announcer saying, "We have confirmed that President John F. Kennedy has been shot while traveling through Dallas, and that he is now dead. We repeat: President John F. Kennedy is dead." (12)I was shocked. (13)I could not believe what I had heard, so I listened more carefully. (14)They repeated the information.

(15)When I realized it was true, I immediately left the library and returned to the orchestra rehearsal. (16)I had to tell someone! (17)I went back to the orchestra room, where the other students were still rehearsing. (18)Before I had a chance to interrupt the rehearsal, the principal of the school made an announcement on the public address system. (19)Suddenly people began crying, and all normal activities came to a halt. (20)The teacher turned on the television and for the next two hours we watched the news reports of the horrifying developments.

EXAMPLE 2:

(1)I will never forget the moment the earthquake struck San Francisco. (2)I was still in my office. (3)I had been trying to finish a project before I left for the day. (4)Suddenly, the building began to sway. (5)Books fell off their shelves. (6)People were screaming. (7)It seemed like things were moving for several minutes, but I guess the actual time was pretty short. (8)As soon as the building had stopped moving, I tried to get out as quickly as possible. (9)This wasn't easy, because I work on the 17th floor, and of course the electricity went out the moment the earthquake struck, so no elevators were working. (10)I ran down the emergency stairs in darkness and got out to the street. (11)Literally hundreds of people were standing around, wondering what to do. (12)Then someone appeared who had a transistor radio, and we all stood as close as we could to him, while he tried to find a news station that could give us information about what had just happened and about what we should do. (13)After about 20 minutes, I realized that all public transportation had stopped, and if I wanted to go home, I would have to walk. (14)When I finally got home, there was no electricity, but the apartment was OK, and my roommate Matt and the dog were both sitting outside. He was talking to the neighbor, and watching the news broadcasts on a portable battery-operated TV. (15)We all sat around and told each other about our experiences.

- Compare your account to other people's stories. In a group, decide on an answer to this question:

    Are there any common feelings or reactions that all or most people share in situations when they hear about or experience some very important or surprising event?

- Present your list of shared reactions to the rest of the class.

Focus 1

FORM

Irregular Verbs

FORM

- Many of the most common verbs in English are irregular. This means that they have separate forms (rather than just adding **-ed**) when you use them in simple past tense or as past participles (with perfect aspect or with passive voice). Because they are so common, it is important to know these forms well.

Exercise 1

The following is a partially completed chart of the most common irregular verbs in English. Check your knowledge of irregular verbs by filling in the blanks to complete the entire chart. You may work with other students to share your knowledge, or you might want to refer to a dictionary for the forms you are not sure of:

Simple Form	Past Tense Form	Past Participle	Simple Form	Past Tense Form	Past Participle
_____	_____	become	_____	_____	dug
begin	_____	_____	do	_____	_____
_____	bent	_____	_____	drew	_____
_____	_____	bet	_____	_____	drunk
bind	_____	_____	drive	_____	_____
_____	bit	_____	_____	ate	_____
_____	_____	bled	_____	_____	fallen
blow	_____	_____	feed	_____	_____
_____	broke	_____	_____	felt	_____
_____	_____	brought	_____	fought	_____
build	_____	_____	find	_____	_____
_____	_____	bought	_____	fit	_____
catch	_____	_____	fly	_____	_____
_____	chose	_____	forbid	_____	_____
come	_____	_____	forget	_____	_____
_____	cost	_____	_____	forgave	_____
cut	_____	_____	_____	_____	frozen

Simple Form	Past Tense Form	Past Participle
get	_____	_____
_____	gave	_____
go	_____	_____
_____	_____	ground
_____	grew	_____
hang	_____	_____
_____	had	_____
hear	_____	_____
_____	hid	_____
_____	_____	hit
_____	held	_____
hurt	_____	_____
_____	kept	_____
_____	_____	known
lead	_____	_____
_____	left	_____
lend	_____	_____
_____	_____	let
make	_____	_____
_____	_____	meant
meet	_____	_____
_____	put	_____
_____	_____	quit

Simple Form	Past Tense Form	Past Participle
read	_____	_____
_____	rode	_____
_____	_____	rung
rise	_____	_____
_____	ran	_____
_____	_____	said
see	_____	_____
_____	sought	_____
_____	_____	sold
send	_____	_____
_____	set	_____
_____	_____	shaken
shine	_____	_____
_____	shot	_____
_____	_____	shut
sing	_____	_____
_____	sank	_____
_____	_____	sat
sleep	_____	_____
_____	slid	_____
_____	_____	spoken
speed	_____	_____
_____	spent	_____

Simple Form	Past Tense Form	Past Participle
_____	_____	split
spread	_____	_____
_____	sprang	_____
_____	_____	stood
steal	_____	_____
_____	stuck	_____
_____	_____	stung
strike	_____	_____
swear	_____	_____
_____	swept	_____
_____	swam	_____
_____	_____	swung
take	_____	_____

Simple Form	Past Tense Form	Past Participle
_____	taught	_____
_____	_____	torn
tell	_____	_____
_____	thought	_____
_____	_____	thrown
understand	_____	_____
_____	woke	_____
_____	_____	worn
weave	_____	_____
_____	wept	_____
_____	_____	won
wind	_____	_____
_____	wrote	_____

Focus 2

Indicating Time Relationships in Past Time Frame

USE

- The Past Time Frame is the most frequently used time frame for narratives (telling stories) or talking about past events. In the Past Time Frame, when discussing more than one related action or event, or when two verbs have the same moment of focus, it is necessary to indicate their time relationship. This can be done
  - by sequence: (Things happen in the order in which they are mentioned.)
    (a) He walked up the stairs. He turned the knob and opened the door.
  - by adverbs and adverbial phrases and clauses:
    (b) As he entered the room, he realized something was different. **Before** he had a chance to turn around, he knew something was missing. **In a moment,** he realized what it was.
  - by aspect markers:
    (c) The television **had disappeared.** The antennae wires **were hanging** from the wall. He **had been watching** TV a few hours earlier, but now there **was** nothing there.
- Speakers and writers of English use a mixture of these methods, but in general they are less likely to use aspect to indicate time relationships if the relationship has also been made clear by sequence, by adverbials, or by general context. Students of English sometimes use aspect markers when they don't really need to, because adverbial information has already made the context clear. Knowing when to use (or not use) aspect markers can be difficult, so the first step in learning about this is to notice how native speakers indicate these differences.

Exercise 2

For each of these passages, list the highlighted verbs in the order that the actions occurred. Tell how you think that the order is indicated (by adverb, sequence, or aspect markers).

EXAMPLE: As he **entered the room,** he realized something was different. Before he **had a chance to turn around,** he **knew something was missing.** In a moment, he **realized** what it was. The television **had disappeared.** The antennae wires **were hanging from the wall. He had been watching TV** a few hours earlier, but now **there was nothing there.**

Order of Events	How Indicated
1. he had been watching television	aspect, adverb (a few hours earlier)
2. the television had disappeared	aspect
3. the wires were hanging	aspect
4. there was nothing there	adverb(now)
5. he entered the room	adverb (as)
6. he knew something was missing	sequence
7. he had a chance to turn around	adverb (before)
8. he realized what it was	sequence

1. Police **reported** yesterday that they **had uncovered** a large cache of stolen goods from a warehouse in the southern part of the city. The warehouse **had been** under surveillance for some time. A suspiciously large number of people **had been seen** going in and out of the storage facility. Once the police **had obtained** a search warrant, they **entered** the building in the middle of the night and **discovered** large amounts of electronic equipment and building supplies. Police **announced** that this discovery **might lead** to the solution of a number of robberies.

2. At the time of the earthquake, Jeff **was** still in his office. He **had been trying** to finish a project before he left for the day. Suddenly, the building **began** to sway. Books **fell** off their shelves. People **were screaming.** Although it seemed as if things were moving for several minutes, the actual time was just 15 seconds.

   Even before the building **stopped** moving, people **were trying** to get out as quickly as possible. This wasn't easy for people who **had been working** in the higher floors of the building. The electricity **had gone off** the moment the earthquake struck, so no elevators **were working.** Most people **ran** down emergency stairs in darkness and got out to the street.

Exercise 3

What is the time relationship between the highlighted verbs in each of the numbered sentences in this passage? How is the time relationship indicated? By sequence? By adverbials? By aspect? By both? The first sentence has been done for you as an example.

> EXAMPLE: first action: *had been looking;*
>
> second action: *broke out;*
>
> how indicated: *aspect and adverbial (before)*

(1) Even before the disastrous fire that destroyed large portions of Imperial Rome **broke out,** the Emperor Nero **had been looking** for ways to control or eliminate the growing Christian population in the city. (2) When news of the fire **reached** the emperor's palace, he **became** quite jubilant. (3) He obviously **had been looking** for some excuse, and now he **had** one, made to order. He went immediately to the roof of the palace. The city was a sea of flames all around him. (4) In spite of the fact that people **were screaming** for their lives on the streets below, Nero **ordered** that a lyre be brought to him at once. (5) He **decided** to compose a poem comparing the destruction of Rome to that of Troy in Homer's *Iliad,* and **began** singing.

(6) However, contrary to the common saying, Nero **did not fiddle** while Rome burned, because the fiddle—or violin, as it is more commonly known—**had not yet been invented.** But he did stand on the roof of the palace, and he was heard singing and playing a musical instrument. (7) The actual origins of the fire **were never determined,** but modern scholars agree that the Christian community **had not been** responsible for the destruction of the city. (8) However, the fire **provided** Nero with the excuse he **had been looking for,** and the next day Imperial Troops **began** to round up groups of Christians and take them off to prison.

Focus 3

USE

When, While, and Progressive Aspect

USE

- With most time adverbials, the relationship is clear, but certain adverbs do not give enough information, and you **must** use aspect to express the time relationship.

When indicates that the verb happened **before or at the same time as the moment of focus**.	*While* indicates that the action was **in progress at the moment of focus.**
(a) When Nero heard about the fire, he ran to the roof of the palace.	**(b)** Nero played the violin **while** Rome burned.

- If you use *when* to connect an action that is already in progress with the moment of focus, you **must** use progressive aspect.

	Implied Meaning
When the fire broke out, Nero **persecuted** the Christians.	First the fire happened, then Nero persecuted the Christians.
When the fire broke out, Nero **was persecuting** the Christians.	Nero started persecuting the Christians before the fire happened.

Exercise 6

Work with a partner. Take turns asking and answering these questions about the example passages in the Task. What does this activity tell you about the difference between simple past and past progressive tenses? Present your ideas to the rest of the class.

PASSAGE 1:

1. What was the writer doing when he heard the news about J.F.K.?
2. What did the writer do when he heard the news about J.F.K?
3. What were his classmates in the orchestra doing when they heard the news about J.F.K?
4. What did they do when they heard the news about J.F.K?

PASSAGE 2:

1. What was Jeff doing when the building started to sway?
2. What did Jeff do when the building stopped swaying?
3. What happened to the elevators when the earthquake struck?
4. What was happening when Jeff reached the street?
5. What happened when Jeff reached the street?
6. What was happening when Jeff finally got home?
7. What happened when Jeff finally got home?

Focus 4

Other Uses of Progressive Aspect

USE

- Even though a time relationship is clear, a speaker / writer may decide to also use progressive aspect to indicate these kinds of additional information:
  - to emphasize "in progress" or "uncompleted":
    - **(a)** In 1967, while I **was researching** the economic consequences of the American Civil War, I came upon a fascinating piece of information.
  - repetition or duration:
    - **(b)** During the last few years of his life, Mozart **was constantly trying** to borrow money from anyone who would loan it to him.
  - temporary situation:
    - **(c)** When John first got to Paris, he **was staying for a short while** at the house of a shopkeeper and his family.

Exercise 7

Identify all the past progressive verb forms in the example passages of the Task and tell why you think the author chose to use past progressive.

Exercise 8

Choose the appropriate form of the verbs indicated in the passage below. There may be more than one correct choice, so prepare to explain why you chose the form you did. The first sentence has been done for you as an example.

(1) The St. Lawrence Seaway, the waterway that ((links) / is linking) the Great Lakes of North America with the Atlantic Ocean, was discovered by explorers who (looked / (were looking)) for the Northwest Passage. (2) Geographers at that time (believed / were believing) that there was a water course that (connected / was connecting) the Atlantic and Pacific oceans. (3) Throughout the sixteenth and early seventeenth centuries, both England and France constantly (sent / were sending) one expedition after another to find the passage. (4) Early explorers (investigated / were investigating) virtually every large inlet and river along the entire Eastern coast of North America.

(5) Even though they never (found / were finding) the Northwest Passage, these early explorers (made / were making) a valuable contribution to the knowledge of North American geography. (6) While they (explored / were exploring) the coast, they (made / were making) many other very useful discoveries. (7) Not only the St. Lawrence, but also Hudson Bay, Chesapeake Bay, the Hudson River, and the Delaware River all (were discovered / were being discovered) by explorers who actually (looked / were looking) for something else.

Focus 5

Using Perfect Aspect in Past Time

USE

- You can use both adverbials and aspect markers to indicate that something happened before the moment of focus.

Adverbials	Aspect
Before we left on the trip, we checked the car thoroughly. **After** we checked the oil, we made sure the tires had enough air.	But we **hadn't gotten** more than a few miles when we realized that we **had forgotten** something: We **had left** our suitcases on the front porch. We **had been worrying** so much about the mechanical condition of the car that we left without thinking about its contents.

- However, native speakers do not typically use both. They sometimes tend to avoid the past perfect tense if the time sequence is clear from other information in the passage, and use it only when it is necessary to communicate a logical connection between the two events, to clarify the time relationship, or to change the moment of focus in indirect speech.
- A writer/speaker may decide to use perfect aspect, even when the time relationship is made clear by adverbs or sequence, to indicate
  - the action was fully completed:

    (a) I **had finished** all my homework **before** I went to Jane's party.
  - a strong logical connection:

    (b) He **had seen** the movie, and **therefore** didn't want to go with us.

401

Exercise 9

Examine how adverbials and aspect are used to indicate time relationships. For each sentence in these passages, identify the moment of focus and list the verbs that happened before the moment of focus in the order that they occurred. Are the time relationships indicated by adverbials, by aspect, or by both? The first two sentences in each passage have been done for you as an example.

(1)Before we left on the trip, we checked the car thoroughly. (2)After we checked the oil, we made sure the tires had enough air. (3)But we hadn't gotten more than a few miles when we realized that we had forgotten something: We had left our suitcases on the front porch. (4)We had been worrying so much about the mechanical condition of the car that we left without thinking about its contents.

Moment of Focus	Time Before	How Indicated
1) we left on the trip	we checked the car	adverb(before)
2) we made sure the tires had enough air	we checked the oil	adverb(after)

The fifteenth century saw the emergence of a new social and economic order in Europe. (1)By the end of the fourteenth century, the population of Europe was about a third smaller than it had been at the beginning. (2)It was one of the few times in history when the population had not only stopped growing but had actually decreased. (3)This smaller population was caused by repeated outbreaks of bubonic plague that had swept through the continent several times during the century, (4)and when the century ended, this had resulted in some fundamental changes in society. (5)So many people had died that the traditional feudal landlords were forced to intermarry with wealthy merchant families, rather than aristocratic ones. (6)People who had previously only had the opportunity to make a living as farmers or serfs were able to become craftsmen and artisans. (7)The plague had killed so many people that the traditional social boundaries were wiped out, and this created a period of great social mobility and economic change.

Moment of Focus	Time Before	How Indicated
1) the population was one-third smaller	than it had been	adverbial (by the end of the fourteenth-century)
2) It was one of the few times in history	the population had stopped growing / had decreased	aspect

Exercise 10

Use the **past perfect** in the following sentences only if it is necessary to the meaning of the sentence. Otherwise use the **simple past** or **past progressive.**

1. Because Nero _____ (want) an excuse to persecute the Christians, he told everyone that they _____ (start) the fire.

2. Peter _____ (go) to talk with Mr. Green about the fight he _____ (have) with Denise earlier in the day.

3. As soon as the building _____ (stop moving), Jeff _____ (try) to call Matt, but the telephones _____ (stop working).

4. It was too late to put out the fire because it _____ (grow) too big for anything to control.

5. I _____ (look) everywhere for my wallet, but I _____ (not find) it anywhere. It _____ (disappear).

6. When the radio _____ (announce) that President Kennedy _____ (be shot), all normal activities _____ (come) to a halt.

7. Denise _____ (go) to Peter's office to complain about his attitude, but he _____ (leave) early to take his children to the circus.

8. Mary _____ (be) extremely worried about John since she _____ (not receive) any letters from him in over a month.

Focus 6

Perfect Progressive Aspect in Past Time

USE

- An author may decide to use perfect progressive aspect in addition to adverbs or where the time sequence is already clear to give additional information about the verb:
  - continuous action rather than repeated action:

(a) It **had been snowing for three hours.** Unless they cleared the roads soon, it was likely that we would have to spend the night in our car.	(b) It **had snowed several times** since we arrived, but there still wasn't enough snow to ski.

- uncompleted action rather than completed action:

(c) I **had been visiting** my aunt, when she suddenly became quite ill and asked me to drive her to the hospital.	(d) I **had visited** my aunt, so I was free to spend the rest of the afternoon at the museum.

Exercise 11

Decide whether **past perfect** or **past perfect progressive** is the appropriate tense for the verbs in the blanks.

1. When the earthquake struck, Jeff was still in the office because he _____ (try) to finish a project before he left for the day.

2. Emperor Nero _____ (look) for a reason to arrest Christians even before the fire that destroyed much of Rome.

3. By the beginning of the 15th Century, the Bubonic Plague _____ (cause) some fundamental social and political changes.

4. The police _____ (keep) the warehouse under surveillance for some time when they finally obtain a search warrant and investigated.

5. They first became suspicious because so many people _____ (go) in and out of the warehouse at strange hours of the day and night.

Exercise 12

Decide whether the verbs below should be in past tense, past perfect, or past perfect progressive. More than one answer may be correct, so prepare to explain why you chose the tense you did.

1. I _____ (work) in the library for about 20 minutes when I _____ (overhear) the radio broadcast announcing Kennedy's assassination.

2. Jeff _____ (experience) several minor earthquakes, but he _____ (be) still surprised by the strength of this one.

3. Bob _____ (be) not really happy with what he _____ (do), so he _____ (decide) to look for another job.

4. European explorers _____ (try) to reach Asia when they _____ (land) in the New World "by accident."

5. When Jeff _____ (get) to the street, he _____ (see) that hundreds of other people _____ (leave) their offices and _____ (stand) out on the street wondering what to do.

Exercise 13

Decide on the correct verb tense (present, present perfect, simple past, past perfect, past progressive, or past perfect progressive) for the verbs in the blanks. There may be more than one correct answer, so prepare to explain why you made the choice you did.

(1)George Washington _____ (be) the first President of the United States, and

_____ (serve) as the leader of American troops during the War of Independence.

(2)According to a famous story, one year, when George _____ (be) a young boy,

and _____ (learn) how to use farming tools, his father _____ (give) him a

hatchet for his birthday. (3)George _____ (be) anxious to use the hatchet, so he

_____ (run) out of the house and _____ (chop) down a cherry tree in his

father's garden. (4)When his father _____ (discover) that someone _____

(chop) down the tree, he _____ (be) furious. (5)He _____ (demand) to know

who _____ (chop) down his cherry tree. (6)When Little George _____ (hear)

his father's angry shouting, he _____ (go) to his father and _____ (tell) him

that he _____ (do) it with his new hatchet. (7)He said, "I _____ (be) sorry

you _____ (are) angry, and I _____ (know) you will punish me, but I must

admit my crime, because I cannot tell a lie." (8)George's father _____ (be) so im-

pressed with his honesty, that he _____ (decide) not to punish the boy after all,

and, in fact,_____ (reward) him, by giving him a silver dollar.

(9)This story actually never _____ (happen), but millions of American children

_____ (read) this story in school. (10)Parents and teachers _____ (think) that

it is a good way to teach children to be honest and to always tell the truth.

Activities

Activity 1

Write a paragraph that tells about a personal experience that happened to you or to someone you know which supports the truth of one of the following proverbs.

An idle mind is the devil's playground.
Too many cooks spoil the broth.
Two heads are better than one.
If at first you don't succeed, try, try again.
Never count your chickens before they have hatched.

Activity 2

Form groups of three to five people. You are going to write a group story—but in a special way. Each person should take a piece of paper and start a story with this sentence:

"It was a dark and stormy night. Suddenly, (your teacher's name) heard a terrible scream."

Then each person in the group should write for three minutes. When the three minutes are up, fold the paper so that only the last sentence or two can be read. Pass your story to the person on your right, and take the paper of the person on your left. Then each person should write for three minutes to continue that person's story. Repeat the process until the papers have gone completely around the group. Unfold the papers and read the resulting stories to each other.

- Which story has the funniest combination of sentences? Which story has the clearest sequence of activities? Choose the story you like best to read aloud to the rest of the class.

Activity 3

Every country has famous stories in its history that all children learn about when they are growing up. The interesting thing about such stories is that often they are not actually true. In the United States, for example, all schoolchildren have heard the story of George Washington and the Cherry Tree (Exercise 13).

Do you know any similar kinds of famous stories about real people that actually never happened? Write an essay that tells such a story, and why you think the story is told, even though it never happened.

Activity 4

Some historians feel that specific individual people and events do not actually change history but only reflect existing social or political trends. Do you agree or disagree with this theory?

- In a brief essay or oral presentation, choose a famous moment in history (such as Kennedy's assassination, the burning of Rome, or some other event) and describe what happened. Then explain why you think that the incident did or did not actually **cause** the historical developments that followed.

31

Modals in Past Time Frame

Task

How has your personality changed as you have grown older? In what ways are you different than you were in the past?

- Identify some things that you used to do five or ten years ago but don't do anymore. Then identify some things that you do now, but couldn't or wouldn't do five or ten years ago. Compare your list of activities with those of other students in the class.
- Based on the changes you thought of, and those of other students in the class, decide on two general ways that people's lives change for the better as they grow older. Write a brief essay about each area. Use the lists of your previous and current activities to provide examples to support your opinions. Here are two examples (which will also be used in Exercise 2):

EXAMPLE 1:

Growing older makes people more careful about their health. That is certainly true for me.

I used to smoke three packs of cigarettes a day. I would start every morning by lighting a

cigarette and coughing for five minutes. Whenever I walked up a flight of stairs, I would have

to stop halfway up to take a rest. I knew smoking would eventually do serious damage to

my lungs, but I didn't care. I was going to live forever. Besides, I used to think that smoking

made me look sophisticated and mature.

But then I got married, and I had to think about my family. I wasn't going to let cigarettes

make my wife a widow! I was afraid I wouldn't live long enough to see my grandchildren

grow up. So I quit smoking and took up running. When I first started, I couldn't run more

than a few hundred yards before I had to rest. But I knew it would only get easier, and the

longer I quit smoking the faster I was able to run. Now I can run a mile in eight minutes.

I'm in much better shape now than I used to be.

EXAMPLE 2:

Growing older makes people less worried about what other people think. In high school, I used to be really shy. I would avoid talking to people and I couldn't express my ideas in class without feeling very uncomfortable. I guess I was afraid that people were going to laugh at me, or that they would think I was strange. In high school, people were supposed to "fit in." They weren't allowed to be different. So I used to wear the same kind of clothes and try to behave the same way as everybody else. I felt I had to be "one of the crowd."

Now that I am older, I can stand up in front of other people and tell them what I think. I certainly couldn't do that in high school. I wear clothes because I like them, not because other people like them. I think I'm much more independent and self-confident than I used to be in high school.

Focus 1

Overview of Modals in Past Time Frame

**FORM
MEANING**

- The use of one-word and phrasal modals in the Past Time Frame is similar to their use in the Present and Future Time Frames, but there are some different uses and possible forms. This chart shows common modal meanings and forms in Past Time Frame.

MODALS IN PAST TIME

Meaning	One Word Modals	Examples	Phrasal Modals	Examples
necessity	*(No one-word modals for these uses)*		*had to*	**(a)** I **had to** do my homework before we went to the movies.
permission			*was allowed to*	**(b)** John **was allowed to** bring a guest.
advisability/ obligation			*was supposed to*	**(c)** You **were supposed to be** at the doctor's office at 2:00.
ability	*could/couldn't*	**(d)** John **could** speak French when he was younger.	*was able to*	**(e)** I **was able to** get tickets to the concert.
habitual actions	*would/wouldn't*	**(f)** When he lived in France, he **would** always have wine with his meals.	*used to*	**(g)** He **used to** play tennis, but he doesn't anymore.
future events in past time	*would/wouldn't* *might/might not*	**(h)** Naomi hoped that she **would** have the kind of vacation where she **might** meet someone and fall in love.	*was going to/ was about to/ was to*	**(i)** Nora **was about to** leave for the airport. She **was going to** spend a couple of months in Japan.

Exercise 1

It is important to be able to recognize when modals refer to the Present or Future Time Frame and when they refer to the Past Time Frame. Decide whether the following sentences are **a)** requests or **b)** questions about past habits and abilities.

1. Could you tell me how to get to Carnegie Hall?
2. Would you cry when your mother punished you?
3. Could you ride your bicycle to work last week?
4. Would you mind putting out that cigar?
5. Do you think you could tell that joke without laughing?
6. Would you pretend you could fly when you were a child?

Exercise 2

Underline modal forms in the example paragraphs in the Task. Identify the meaning by writing a letter: *(a)* necessity; *(b)* permission; *(c)* advisability; *(d)* ability; *(e)* habitual action; *(f)* future event over each one-word or phrasal modal you have underlined.

Focus 2

MEANING

Permission, Necessity, and Advisability

MEANING

- You cannot use one-word modals to talk about **permission, necessity,** or **advisability** in the Past Time Frame. You must use phrasal modals to express those meanings.

  When I was a child, my brothers and sisters and I **had to** do a number of routine chores. We **were supposed to** keep our rooms clean, and if we didn't, we **weren't allowed to** watch TV until everything was clean and orderly. We **had to** wash the dishes. I **was supposed** to wash them on Mondays, but sometimes I **was allowed** to switch nights with my sister when I **had to** do a lot of homework.

Exercise 3

Write five statements about things you **were allowed to do** when you were a child. Write five statements about things you **were not allowed to do.**

Exercise 4

Find a partner and ask if he or she was allowed to do the things you wrote about in Exercise 3.

> **EXAMPLE:** *When you were a child, were you allowed to stay out after dark?*

Identify some privileges that were the same for both of you, and some that were different. Report your findings to the rest of the class.

Exercise 5

Make five statements about things that you **had to do** when you were a child. Make five statements about things that you **were supposed to do** when you were a child but did not always do.

Exercise 6

Follow the same process in working with a partner that you used in Exercise 4 to report your findings from Exercise 5.

Focus 3

MEANING

Ability in Past Time Frame
Could versus *Was Able To*

MEANING

- You can use both *could* and *was/were able to* to talk about abilities in Past Time Frame.

(a) When Jeanne was a child, she **could** speak excellent French, but she **couldn't** speak English. **Could** you speak any other languages as a child? Yes, I **could** speak a little Italian.	**(b) Were** you **able to** go to Joan's party? No, I **wasn't.** But I **was able to** send her a birthday card.

- Their use depends on whether they refer to a general ability or a specific ability.

General Ability (skills that exist over time)	Specific Ability (specific events or actions)
(c) John **could speak** French,	so he **was able to find** us a hotel in Paris.
(d) John **was able to speak** French,	but he **couldn't find** us a hotel anywhere.
(e) John **couldn't ride** a bike,	so he **wasn't able to join** us on our ride.
(f) John **wasn't able to ride** a bike,	but he **was able to enjoy** the picnic anyway.

- In statements of general ability, there is no difference in meaning or use between *could* and *was able to.* In statements of specific ability, if you use *could*, it must be negative.
  - **(g)** AWKWARD: **Could** you get tickets for the concert? (This sounds like a request in Present Time.)
  - **(h)** NOT: I **could** get two tickets to the concert.
  - **(i)** OK: I stood in line for over an hour, but I **couldn't** get any.

Exercise 7

Decide whether the following statements refer to general ability or specific ability.

1. George was able to get tickets to the play.
2. However, he couldn't find them when it was time to go to the theater.
3. Peter could convince his boss to let him do anything he wanted.
4. As a result, he was able to stay home from work last week.
5. Professor Smith could speak Russian.
6. Because of this, she was able to translate the Foreign Minister's speech to the U.N.
7. Bambang couldn't pass the TOEFL, so he enrolled in an English course.
8. Bambang wasn't able to pass the TOEFL last semester, but he succeeded this semester.

Exercise 8

Here is a list of activities. From this list, identify things that you were able to do ten years ago. Write complete sentences that describe those abilities. Identify things that you couldn't do ten years ago and write complete sentences about them.

Think of three to five other original things for each category and write sentences about them. You should have a total of eight sentences that describe things you could do ten years ago, and eight sentences about things you couldn't do ten years ago.

ride a bike	buy alcoholic beverages
speak fluent English	run a mile in eight minutes
understand American films	drive a truck
play a musical instrument	live independently away from home
read and write English	attend university classes
speak a second language	swim
read and write a second language	play American football
drive a car	translate things into English

Exercise 9

Underline the structures that refer to past abilities in these short passages. Why do you think the author decided to use the particular form he did?

1. Matt stood in line for four hours, but he wasn't able to get tickets for the Grateful Dead concert. When he got home, Jeff could tell that he was frustrated and a little angry. He wanted to cheer Matt up, but he couldn't do much to improve Matt's mood.

2. Billy was a genius. He was able to do many things that other children his age couldn't do. He could solve complicated mathematical equations. He could write poetry and quote Shakespeare. He was even able to get into college when he was only 14 years old. But he couldn't make friends with other children his own age.

Focus 4

MEANING

Habitual Actions: *Would* versus *Used To*

MEANING

- You can use ***would*** and ***used to*** to describe habits and regular activities in the past.
  - **(a)** I **used to** live in Washington, D.C. Every day I **would** go jogging past all the famous monuments. No matter how hot or cold it was, I **would** run around the Tidal Basin and along the Mall.
- Use of these forms depends on whether they describe a habitual **activity** or a habitual **state.**

Activities can be expressed by both ***would*** and ***used to.***	**States** must be expressed by **used to** or simple past tense. We do not use ***would.***
(b) When I was a child, **I would wait** at the bus stop for my father to come home. **(c)** When I was a child, **I used to wait** at the bus stop.	**(d)** When I was a child, I **used to have** lots of toys. **(e)** When I was a child, I **had** lots of toys. **(f)** NOT: When I was a child, I **would have** lots of toys.

Exercise 10

Here is a list of things many children do:

believe in ghosts
be afraid of the dark
eat vegetables
play Cowboys and Indians
pretend to be able to fly
ride a bicycle
spend the night at a friend's house

have a secret hiding place
play with dolls
like going to the doctor
enjoy going to school
obey older brothers or sisters
cry when hurt

1. From this list choose five things that you used to do when you were a child.
2. Choose five things that you did not do.
3. Think of three original things for each category.
4. Write complete sentences describing those activities. Be sure to use the correct form for all stative verbs. You should have eight sentences describing things you used to do as a child and eight sentences about things you did not do.

Exercise 11

Ask a partner questions about the things you wrote about in Exercise 10.

> **EXAMPLE:** *When you were a child, did you ever pretend that you could fly?*

Report some of your partner's answers to the rest of the class.

Focus 5

FORM ● USE

Future in Past Time

FORM
USE

- The Past Time Frame can include references to future events. The actual time of these events may be in the past in relation to *now* (the moment of speaking or writing), but it is in the future in relation to our moment of focus.
  - **(a)** My parents **got married** over 50 years ago. **In 1937**, my father first met the woman that he **would** marry a few years later. From that very first day, my father knew that he **was** eventually **going to** marry her.
  - **(b)** Although Lincoln **wasn't to become** President until 1860, he started running for political offices quite early in his career. He **would have** three unsuccessful tries at public office before he finally won his first election.

415

Exercise 12

Underline all the modal structures that refer to future events or intentions in these paragraphs.

(1) When I was a child, I used to dream about my future. (2) I thought I was going to be a doctor or a movie star. (3) I would have a university medical degree. (4) I would have a job where I could do what I wanted, and I wouldn't have to go to an office every day. (5) I was going to be famous, and I was definitely going to have lots of money. (6) I would have a big house in Hollywood and ten children.

(1) Nora was going to spend a month in Japan before she started her new job, which was to begin in six weeks. (2) She was going to fly to Japan last Monday, but a strange thing happened as she was about to leave for the airport. (3) Suddenly she had a strong sensation that she shouldn't get on the plane. (4) She had a strange feeling that there might be an accident, or that there would be some other mishap. (5) She knew that she could take a flight later in the week, so that's what she decided to do.

Focus 6

USE

Was Going To versus Would

USE

- You should use *was going to* instead of *would*
  - to introduce a topic:
    (a) Elizabeth didn't have much time to get ready for the prom. She **was going to** do all her errands in a single afternoon. First she **would** pick up her dress. Then she **would** get her hair done. That **would** leave her the rest of the afternoon to get ready.
  - to indicate immediate future:
    (b) John didn't want to leave the house. It **was going to** rain any minute.
  - to describe unfulfilled intentions (intended actions that did not actually take place):
    (c) At first, my parents **weren't going to** let me stay up late, but I convinced them to let me do it.
    (d) Oh, here you are! I **was going to** call you, but now I don't have to.
    (e) We **were going to** go skiing tomorrow, but there's no snow, so we'll just stay home instead.

Exercise 13

Do the following sentences describe **a)** unfulfilled intentions or **b)** future activities? In sentences that describe future activities, substitute *would* for *was/were going to.*

> **EXAMPLE:** Nora and Jim aren't here right now. They said they **were going to** be studying at the library.
>
> *It describes future activity: They said they would be studying at the library.*

1. I **wasn't going to** mention the money you owe me. But since you brought it up, I guess we should talk about it.
2. My teacher **wasn't going to** postpone the test, so we studied for the entire weekend.
3. The committee organized the refreshments for the party. Mary **was going to** bring cookies. John **was going to** take care of beverages.
4. I'm not finished painting the house. Jim **was going to help,** but I guess he had something else to do.
5. **Were you going to** send me a check? I haven't received it yet.
6. I never thought the party **was going to** be this much fun.
7. We **weren't going to** extend our vacation, but the weather was so nice that we decided to stay for a few more days.

Exercise 14

Decide which form, *would* or *was/were going to,* you should use in the following sentences. In some cases, both answers may be correct.

1. As soon as Charley heard about Rebecca's party, he decided that he _____ (not go). Gladys _____ (be) there, and she and Charley didn't get along. He was afraid that she _____ (probably drink) too much and then she _____ (want) to tell everyone about how they used to be engaged to be married.

2. Last week Jeff stood in line for five hours to get a ticket to the opera, but he knew it was worth the long wait. It _____ (be) a great performance. Pavarotti _____ (sing) the part of Falstaff. Jeff had heard him before, so he was sure it _____ (be) wonderful.

3. Naomi didn't know what to do for her vacation. Perhaps she _____ (go) to Mexico. The plane ticket _____ (be) expensive, but she didn't want to travel by herself on the bus.

4. When I talked to Janet last Sunday night, she wasn't planning on getting much sleep. Her project was already a week late, and she couldn't ask the professor for another extension. She _____ (finish) her assignment, even if she had to stay up until dawn. It _____ (not be) easy. She had to finish reading *War and Peace,* and then write a ten-page paper. She _____ (probably be) up all night.

5. We performed a very difficult experiment in our chemistry class the other day. I was very nervous because we had to put just the right amount of chemicals into a solution in order for the reaction to occur. Too much phosphorous _____ (cause) the wrong reaction. If there was too little, nothing _____ (happen) at all. If I _____ (do) the experiment correctly, it _____ (be) necessary to measure very, very carefully.

Exercise 15

For the expressions of Future in Past Time Frame that you found in the passage in Exercise 13, decide why you think the author used one form rather than another.

Activities

Activity 1

In the introductory Task, you talked about ways in which people change for the better as they grow older. Now think about ways that people change for the worse.

- Make a list of things that you can no longer do that you used to be able to do. These may be activities or privileges. If you wish, compare your list to those of other students in the class.
- Write a paragraph describing one general way that people's lives change for the worse as they grow older. Use the list of things you can no longer do to help you organize your thoughts and provide examples for you to support your ideas.

Activity 2

In 1989, important political changes in Eastern Europe resulted in important changes in worldwide economics, politics, and military alliances. In 1991, the outbreak of war in the Middle East caused similar unexpected changes in world affairs.

- What predictions did people make about world events before these changes occurred? What things are happening now that seemed impossible a few years ago? With other students, develop two lists:

  1. things people thought were going to happen that no longer seem likely to happen
  2. things that are happening now that people never thought would happen

  Make a presentation to the rest of the class about great surprises in history or unforseen developments in world affairs.

Activity 3

Write a short paragraph about one or more of these topics:

- bad habits that you used to have but do not have anymore.
- things you would do as a child when you were unhappy.
- a time when you were going to do something but were not allowed or were not able to do so.
- how your life has turned out differently from your expectations (things you thought were going to happen that did not and vice versa).

Activity 4

Science Fiction is a kind of literature that describes how things will be in the future. Writers of science fiction have been making predictions about the future for many years. Jules Verne, H. G. Wells, George Orwell, and Aldous Huxley were all famous writers who wrote novels describing life at the end of the twentieth century. Compare their visions of the future with the way things actually are. Were the writers right or wrong in their portrayals of the future?

- Jules Verne's predictions in *From the Earth to the Moon* and *Twenty Thousand Leagues Under the Sea:*

  Everyone will own an airplane.

  There will be colonies on the moon.

  There will be a single world language.

  People will use solar power to get energy.

- H. G. Wells' predictions in *The War of the Worlds* and other novels:

  Aliens from Mars will invade the earth.

  The aliens will conquer the earth.

  The aliens will succumb to bacterial infections.

  People will be able to travel through time.

  Scientists will discover a chemical that will make people invisible.

- George Orwell's predictions in *1984:*

  The government will control all aspects of people's lives.

  There will only be three or four huge governments, and they will constantly be at war with each other.

  People will be watched by police, by hidden cameras, and microphones.

  Anyone who tries to disagree with the government will be put in prison.

- Aldous Huxley's predictions in *Brave New World*:

  Children will be born through artificial means.

  They will be raised in state-run nurseries, instead of in individual families.

  There will be movies that are so realistic that people will think they are actually happening.

  The use of mind-altering drugs will be widespread, and encouraged by the government.

- Which writer did the most accurate job of predicting the future? Write an essay or make a presentation to the rest of the class on the accurate and mistaken predictions of these famous writers.

Activity 5

How has the social role of women changed in the last 50 years? What things were your grandmothers not allowed to do, simply because they were women? What things would women never consider doing 50 years ago that are commonplace today? Write a paragraph or make a presentation to the rest of the class discussing the five biggest differences between women's lives 50 years ago as compared with today.

Reported Speech

U N I T

32

Task

Look at the following series of pictures. It is the photographic record of a conversation between Jack and Jean.

• What do you think these people are talking about? Write down the exact conversation that you think occurred between them.

PHOTO 1:

    Jack:

    Jean:

    Jack:

    Jean:

PHOTO 2:

    Jack:

    Jean:

    Jack:

PHOTO 3:

Jean:

Jack:

Jean:

PHOTO 4:

Jack:

Jean:

Jack:

Jean:

- Now compare your conversation with that of another student in the class. Discuss what you thought they were talking about in each picture and why you thought that. Your discussion might be something like this:

    You: In the first picture, I thought that Jack was telling Jean that he had something important to tell her.

    Your partner: Oh, really? I thought that he was trying to introduce himself for the first time. Why did you think he already knew her?

    You: Because they're sitting rather close together.

- Report the three most interesting differences between your two conversations (and your reasons for thinking so) to the rest of the class.

MEANING

Basic Time Frame in Direct Quotation and Reported Speech

MEANING

- When people describe a conversation that happened in the past, they often use reported speech rather than direct quotation. **Direct quotation is the actual words that were spoken** in the conversation. **Reported speech** expresses the **meaning** of what was said.

Direct Quotation	Reported Speech
present time frame: **now:** the conversation itself **then:** things that happen before the conversation use past tense. **I/My** = Jack	**past time frame:** **now:** the report of the conversation **then:** the conversation itself **time before then:** Things that happened before the conversation use perfect aspect. **I/My** = Jean **He/his** = Jack
Jack is speaking at this moment: "I'm really sick. I am having terrible headaches. I'm going to try to see my doctor this afternoon, if I can get someone to drive me to his office."	Jean is reporting a conversation with Jack: "I'm worried about Jack. I saw him yesterday. He said that he was really sick. He was having terrible headaches. He was going to try to see his doctor yesterday afternoon, if he could get someone to drive him to the doctor's office. I hope he's O.K.!"
"My headache was getting worse all the time, so I went to the doctor yesterday. She took my temperature. She prescribed some pills. My condition has improved, but I still haven't gone back to work yet."	"I saw Jack yesterday. He's a little better. He said that his headache had been getting worse, so he had gone to the doctor the day before yesterday. She had taken his temperature. She had prescribed some pills. Jack felt that his condition had improved, but he still hadn't gone back to work."

Focus 2

Tense Change in Reported Speech

FORM

- The change in the frame of reference requires changes in form. You need to make changes in verb tenses
  - to refer to the Present Time Frame:

Direct Quotation: Moment of Focus: now Form: present tenses	Reported Speech: Moment of Focus: then Form: past tenses
I'm really sick. I **am having** terrible headaches. **I'm going to try** to see my doctor this afternoon, if I **can get** someone to drive me to his office."	He **was** really sick. He **was having** terrible headaches. He **was going to try** to see his doctor yesterday afternoon, if he **could get** someone to drive him to the doctor's office.

  - to refer to the Past Time Frame:

Moment of Focus: time before now Form: past tense/present perfect	Moment of Focus: time before then Form: past perfect tenses
My headache **was getting** worse all the time, so I **went** to the doctor yesterday. She **took** my temperature. She **prescribed** some pills. My condition **has improved,** but I still **haven't gone** back to work yet.	His headache **had been getting** worse, so he **had gone** to the doctor the day before yesterday. She **had taken** his temperature. She **had prescribed** some pills. Jack felt that his condition **had improved** but when I spoke to him he still **hadn't gone** back to work.

Exercise 1

Denise Driven had a meeting with her boss, Mr. Green, to complain about some of the things that Peter Principle was or was not doing in the office. Listed below are some of the complaints that Denise made about Peter. Change these direct quotations to reported speech, using the cue given:

> **EXAMPLE:** "I've been getting more and more annoyed by Peter's behavior." Denise reported that. . . .
>
> *Denise reported that she had been getting more and more annoyed by Peter's behavior.*

1. "Peter needs to be more serious about work." Denise felt that. . . .
2. "Peter came to work 15 minutes late for the second time in a month." Denise was angry that. . . .
3. "Peter is going to leave the office early to see his child perform in a school play." She complained that. . . .
4. "He is always whistling in the office." She didn't like the fact that. . . .
5. "He has made rude comments about my personal life." She was upset that. . . .

Exercise 2

Listed below are other complaints Denise had about Peter. How do you think she stated her complaints? Restate them as direct quotations, using **"Denise said. . . ."**

> **EXAMPLE:** She reported that she had been getting more and more annoyed by Peter's behavior.
>
> *Denise said, "I have been getting more and more annoyed by Peter's behavior."*

1. She was annoyed that he didn't always finish projects on time.
2. She was unhappy that he told too many jokes at staff meetings.
3. She didn't like the fact that he refused to come into the office on Saturdays.
4. She was upset that he was going to miss an important meeting because he had promised to take his children to the circus.
5. She was angry that he constantly allowed his personal life to interfere with his work obligations.

Focus 3

Modal Changes in Reported Speech

- You need to change present modals to past modals in reported speech:

Direct Quotation	Reported Speech
(a) "I **will try** to see my doctor this afternoon, if I **can** get someone to drive me to his office."	**(b)** He said that he **would try** to see his doctor yesterday afternoon, if he **could** get someone to drive him to the doctor's office.
may changes to	*might*
can	*could*
shall	*should*
will	*would*

- But do not change past modals to perfect modals:

Direct Quotation	Reported Speech
(c) "I **couldn't** get tickets."	**(d)** Jack said that he **couldn't** get tickets.
	(e) NOT: Jack said that he **couldn't have gotten** tickets.

Exercise 3

The following is the response Mr. Green made when he talked with Denise. Change his direct quotation to reported speech. Start your paragraph with: *Mr. Green said that....* Add *Mr. Green suggested that...* and *Mr. Green thought that...* in other places in the paragraph.

> Mr. Green said, "The personnel officer will be asked to speak to Peter. If Peter can't get to the office on time, he will just have to take an earlier bus. He may not be crazy about getting up at 5:30, but he will have to do it if he wants to keep his job. Personnel won't talk to Peter about the other problems he may be having, though. One of Peter's friends in the office can deal with him directly about his lack of responsibility. Peter probably won't change much, but he may be more willing to listen to the complaints if he can get the information from someone he likes and respects."

Focus 4

Changes in Pronouns and Possessive Determiners

FORM

- In reported speech, you must change pronoun and possessive determiners in order to maintain meaning:

	Implied Meaning
(a) Jack said,"**I** am sick."	Jack is sick.
(b) Jack told me that **I** was sick.	I am sick, not Jack.
(c) Jack told me that **he** was sick.	Jack is sick.
Direct Quotation	**Reported Speech**
(d) "**You** will be happy to know that **my** condition has improved, but **I** still haven't gone back to **my** office yet."	**(e)** He said that **I** would be happy to know that **his** condition had improved, but **he** still hadn't gone back to **his** office yet.

- If there is some confusion about what a pronoun or possessive determiner refers to, it may be necessary to substitute the actual noun:

Direct Quotation	Reported Speech
(f) "I asked my brother Peter to bring **his** wife to the party."	**(g)** Jack asked his brother to bring his— **Peter's**—wife to the party.

Focus 5

Changes in Demonstratives and Adverbials

FORM

- You may also need to change demonstratives and adverbials to maintain meaning:

	Implied Meaning
(a) On Saturday, Jack said, "Please come **here** for dinner **tonight**."	Jack wants the speaker to arrive at his house on Saturday.
(b) On Saturday, Jack asked me to go **there** for dinner **that night**.	
(c) On Saturday, Jack asked me to come **here** for dinner **tonight**.	Jack wants the speaker to arrive at the place and time of the second conversation— not Jack's house, not Saturday.
Direct Quotation	**Reported Speech**
(d) "I went to the doctor **yesterday**."	**(e)** Jack told me that he had gone to the doctor **on the previous day**.

- Here are some examples of common changes in reference that reported speech requires:

this/these	changes to	*that/those*
here		*there*
today/tonight		*that day/that night*
yesterday		*the day before/the previous day*
tomorrow		*the next day*
two days from today		*two days from then*
two days ago		*two days earlier*

428

Exercise 4

Change the following statements into reported speech:

> **EXAMPLE:** Jack said, "I came here to see my doctor, but she's on vacation until tomorrow."
>
> *Jack said that he had gone there to see his doctor, but she was on vacation until the next day.*

1. Yesterday morning Peter said, "I am coming to the meeting this afternoon."
2. When I saw Mary last week she told me, "My father may be able to take this letter directly to the Immigration Office later today."
3. Last week my brother told me, "I have already completed all the assignments I have for my classes this week."
4. Two days ago I spoke to the doctor, and she said, "The results of your test will be here by tomorrow morning."
5. Yesterday my mother promised me, "Tomorrow when you come here, I'll give you some of my delicious fudge."

Focus 6

FORM

Statements in Reported Speech

FORM

- In direct quotation, you use the same markers, **quotation marks ("...")**, for statements, questions, and imperatives.

    (a) The doctor told me, "I'm afraid we'll have to do more tests."

    (b) The doctor asked me, "Have you been having these headaches for a long time?"

    In reported speech, different markers are used for statements, questions, and imperatives.

- **That** introduces reported statements. In informal contexts and conversation, **that** is often omitted.

    (c) The doctor told me **that** he was afraid we would have to do more tests.

    (d) The doctor told me he was afraid we would have to do more tests.

Exercise 5

Underline the reported statements in the following passage. Restate each one as direct quotation. Be sure to make the other necessary changes of tense and reference to reflect how the original statements were actually produced. The first one has been done for you as an example.

> **EXAMPLE:** *The representatives announced, "The rate of violent crime has decreased significantly over the last five months."*

(1) At last month's press conference, representatives of the Metropolitan Police Department announced <u>the rate of violent crime had decreased significantly over the last five months.</u> (2) They admitted there had been a slight increase in thefts and burglaries, and that the Department would continue frequent patrols in all neighborhoods. (3) When asked about the budget being discussed with the Mayor's office, they predicted that it would be finalized by the end of that week and that the accelerated hiring program might begin as soon as the following Wednesday.

Exercise 6

Underline the reported statements in the following passage. Restate each one as a direct quotation. Be sure to make the other necessary changes of tense and reference to reflect the exact words that the child actually heard or thought. The first one has been done for you as an example.

> **EXAMPLE:** *His parents told him, "We found you under a cabbage leaf."*

(1) When I was a child, I had some very strange ideas about where babies come from. (2) My parents always told me <u>that they had found me under a cabbage leaf.</u> (3) I knew that probably wasn't true, since I realized there were lots of new babies in my neighborhood and no cabbage plants at all. (4) For several years, I thought my parents had actually bought my younger sister at the hospital. (5) I figured hospitals were places that sold babies to any couple that wanted one. (6) This was because when my mother came back from the hospital after giving birth to my sister, I heard her remind my father that he had to be sure to pay the bill before that week was over. (7) I was a little jealous of my new sister, and I hoped that my father would forget to pay and that the hospital would decide to take her back and sell her to someone else. (8) It wasn't until several years later that I found out that babies were neither bought nor found.

Focus 7

FORM
Questions in Reported Speech

- You need to mark questions in reported speech with two kinds of changes:
  - Changes in word order: All reported speech occurs in statement word order, whether it is a statement or a question.

Direct Quotation:	Reported Speech:
(a) "Am I late?"	**(b)** Jack asked **if he was late.**
(c) "Do you need money?"	**(d)** Jack wanted to know **whether I needed money.**
(e) "How much do you need?"	**(f)** He asked **how much I needed**.

- Addition of question markers:

Yes/no Questions:	
(g) He wanted to know **if** I could bring my notes to the meeting. **(h)** He wanted to know **whether** I could bring my notes to the meeting. **(i)** He wanted to know **whether or not** I could bring my notes to the meeting.	We use **if/whether(or not)** to report "**yes/no**" and "**either/or**" questions. **If** is preferred for "**yes/no**" questions. **Whether(or not)** is preferred for "**either/or**" questions, but both forms can be used in both kinds of questions.

Wh-Questions:	
(j) I applied for a job. They wanted to know **where I lived, when I was born, how many brothers and sisters I had,** and **what kind of previous experience I had had in sales.**	We use a **wh-question word** to report wh- questions.

Exercise 7

Below is a list of interview questions that were common in American businesses 30 or 40 years ago. Employers these days no longer ask some of these questions. In other cases, the law prohibits asking such questions.

1. Are you married or single?
2. Does your wife work outside the home?
3. How many children do you have?
4. Are you a Communist?
5. Do you go to church?
6. How old are you?
7. Why do you want to work for this company?
8. Do you use drugs?
9. What is your racial background?
10. How much experience do you have?

Restate these questions as statements about old-fashioned hiring practices by adding such reporting phrases as, "A number of years ago employers used to ask, . . . " "They wanted to know, . . . " "They often asked prospective employees to tell them, . . . " and other similar phrases you can think of. Which questions do you think are still in use today?

Exercise 8

Read the following report of a job interview. Then write the list of questions the interviewer actually asked.

EXAMPLE: *Where did you go to high school?*

(1)Bob applied for a summer job as a computer programmer in a large company. (2)The head of the Personnel Office interviewed him. (3)She wanted to know where he had graduated from high school, and if he had ever studied in a college or university. (4)She wanted to know if he had ever been arrested, or whether he had ever needed to borrow money in order to pay off credit card purchases. (5)She wanted to know how fast he could type and what kind of experience he had had with computers, and whether he was more proficient in COBOL or BASIC. (6)She asked him what companies he had worked for in the past. (7)She wanted to know what his previous salary had been. (8)She wanted to know why he was no longer working at his previous job. (9)She asked him if he would voluntarily take a drug test. (10)He began to wonder if he really wanted to work for a company that wanted to know so much about his private life.

Focus 8

Commands and Requests in Reported Speech

- Use indirect objects and infinitive complements to report commands and requests.
  - To report **commands**, use verbs like **_tell, order_**, etc. To report **requests**, use verbs such as **_ask, request_**, etc.

    (a) The teacher **told me to do** the homework.

    (b) My roommate **asked me to help** with the dishes.
  - Report negative commands and requests with **not + infinitive**.

    (c) The teacher told me **not to joke** with other students.

    (d) My roommate asked me **not to play** my stereo too loud.

Exercise 9

Rewrite the following indirect commands and requests as direct quotations.

> **EXAMPLE:** On his first day in the Army, Kilroy was told to report to the drill field by the master sergeant.
>
> *The master sergeant told Kilroy, "Report to the drill field."*

1. Another officer assigned him to clean the area for nearly an hour.
2. The officers ordered all the new recruits not to talk to each other.
3. They were told to stand at attention until their papers had been processed.
4. Kilroy asked to go to the bathroom, but this request was denied.
5. Finally the processing was over, and they were ordered to return to their barracks.
6. Several other recruits invited Kilroy to join them in a game of cards.
7. He told them he was too tired, and asked them not to be too noisy, since he wanted to sleep.

Focus 9

When No Tense Changes Are Required

FORM

- You do not need to make the tense and modal changes if you are reporting
  - things that are always true:

(a) My father always told me, "Time **is** money."	**(b)** My father always told me that time **is** money.

- things that are still true:

(c) Jean told me, "Jack **is still living** with his parents after all these years."	**(d)** Jean told me (that) Jack **is still living** with his parents after all these years.

- hypothetical statements:

(e) Peter said, "If I **had** the money, I **would make** a donation to the club, but I **am** a little short on cash this month."	**(f)** Peter said that if he **had** the money, he **would make** a donation to the club, but that he **was** a little short on cash this (last) month.

- statements that occurred only a very short time ago:

(g) Bambang told me, "I **can't** understand a word you're saying."	**(h)** He **just** said that he **can't** understand a word **you're** saying.

- statements where such a change would alter the meaning:

(i) Jack said, "I **could** speak Spanish when I was a child."	**(j)** Jack said that he **could** speak Spanish when he was a child.
	(k) NOT: Jack said that he **could have** spoken Spanish. (This means he had the ability but didn't do it.)

434

Exercise 10

Decide whether tense changes are required for all the verb phrases in the following sentences, if they are changed to reported speech. If a tense change is not required, state the reason why.

EXAMPLE: Shakespeare once observed, "Love is blind."
No change. Timeless truth—still true.
Last week our teacher reminded us, "You should do your homework before you come to class tomorrow."
Last week our teacher reminded us to do our homework before we came to class the next day.

1. A student in my geography class reported, "Not all the people who live in China speak Chinese as their first language."
2. My brother told me, "I wouldn't need to borrow money from you all the time if I had a better-paying job."
3. It was only a minute ago that I asked, "Are you paying attention?"
4. John told me, "I couldn't get any tickets for the concert."
5. Yesterday Denise said "If I were you, I would plan things a little more completely before you leave for vacation next week."
6. This morning Peter told me, "I'm still having problems with Denise, but I'm trying extra hard to get along with her."

Focus 10

USE

Using Reported Speech versus Direct Quotation

USE

- You can use reported speech patterns
  - when you report conversations held earlier:
    (a) No wonder Denise looks sad. I heard that she wouldn't be taking a vacation after all. Apparently, something has come up that makes it impossible for her to leave.
  - when you report things that were thought or believed but not necessarily spoken:
    (b) When he reached the New World, Christopher Columbus **thought** that he had reached Asia, so he called the inhabitants he found there "Indians."
    (c) When I was a little boy, I **was very curious about** whether or not there were dogs in heaven.
  - to make questions or requests more polite:
    (d) Can you tell me **what your ZIP code is?**
    (e) Do you know **what time the store opens?**
    (f) I wonder **if Dr. Jones is able to come to the phone.**

To most native speakers, *yes/no* and *Wh*-questions sound more polite if they are embedded in a conversational frame such as, "Do you know," "Can you tell me," or "I wonder. . . ." Such embedded questions usually have a present time frame, and so the tense of the embedded question does not need to be changed.

- in most formal expository prose:
  - **(g)** I will never forget the day my father told me that the family had decided that I could go to the United States to complete my studies.
  - **(h)** AWKWARD: I will never forget the day my father said, "The family has decided that you can go to the United States to complete your studies."
- You will find direct quotation primarily in narrative fiction and popular non-fiction such as magazine articles, where the author uses quotations of experts to support a point. For most story-telling, direct quotation is more acceptable.

Exercise 11

Identify the examples of reported speech in the following passages and tell why you think the author chose to use (or not to use) reported speech. Discuss your ideas with a partner and present them to the rest of the class.

1. Shakespeare once observed that love is blind. My friend Charley is certainly living proof of that. Six months ago he told me that he had finally met the woman of his dreams. But she doesn't appear to be interested in any of the things that he likes to do. He still comes alone to the bowling club and the soup kitchen. All his friends have noticed that he still seems single on Saturday nights. I thought people who are in love were supposed to enjoy being together.

2. I wonder if you know how I can get in touch with Mona. Do you happen to know where she is living these days? She's moved, and I don't have her new address.

3. People used to think that breathing night air was very unhealthy. Doctors in the Middle Ages actually recommended that people should close all windows when they slept, even in the hottest weather.

4. It was a dark and stormy night. Jason heard a voice whispering on the steps outside. "Your life is in greatest peril," said the voice. But when he looked out the window, there was no one there.

5. I got some rather shocking news yesterday. I heard that a friend of mine had been put in jail for stealing money from her office. She had apparently embezzled thousands of dollars. Of course, I wondered whether she was guilty or not. I still do. I suppose that it could be possible. But I don't really think Denise would do such a thing.

Activities

Activity 1

Work with a different partner from the one with whom you worked on the Task. Together write a conversation that matches the photos in the Task. Act out your conversation for the rest of the class. Other students should write a paraphrase of your conversation.

Activity 2

To *eavesdrop* means to listen secretly to someone else's conversation. Go to a public place, like a restaurant, a shopping mall, or a bus station, and eavesdrop on someone's conversation. It is important not to let people know what you are doing, so pretend to read a book, study your English grammar, read a magazine in another language (people might think that you don't understand English), or pretend to write a letter.

Afterward, try to remember what the people were talking about, and what they said to each other. Did you learn anything interesting about their lives, or about English, as a result of this experience?

Activity 3

Listen to a news broadcast on television. Report one story that you heard on that broadcast to the rest of the class. Start with some sort of statement like this: I heard on the news that . . . , It was announced that . . . , and so on.

Activity 4

Play a game of Telephone. Form two or more teams of ten people each. Student 1 should make a statement to Student 2 very quietly so that only Student 2 can hear what was said. Student 2 then reports what was said to Student 3, using indirect speech ("Student 1 told me that . . . "). Student 3 tells Student 4, and so forth. When the last student receives the report, he or she should announce the message to the rest of the class. Compare how close that message is with what was originally said by Student 1. The team that has the closest, most accurate report wins a point. Student 2 starts the next round.

Activity 5

Write a paragraph discussing some of the misconceptions about life that you had when you were a child. Describe what you thought, and why you thought it. See Exercise 6 for an example.

Activity 6

Tell about a time when you had an important conversation with someone. Perhaps you learned some important information about yourself or someone else. Perhaps you found out about a decision that had a big effect on your life in some way. Perhaps you got some valuable advice.

- First, tell the **story** of the conversation. Write down who it was with and where, and when it took place. Then try to write the conversation word for word.
- Next, write a paragraph telling what you learned from this conversation and why it was important for you. You may want to begin your paragraph with, **"When I was . . . , I learned that. . . . "**

Index